Intentional Dating

How to Stop Dating by Default and Attract Your Best Life Partner

Enjoy!
Sophie Venable
xo

SOPHIE VENABLE, MA

For my daughters, Julia and Natalie, who always encourage me to get my message out there.

I love you infinity!

Contents

Introduction

● ● ● ● ● ●

As we grow into adulthood, we are told we need to worry about where we go to school, what we do for work and where and at what lifestyle we are going to live. We are rarely taught how to choose the one major influencing factor that can, and does, affect every aspect of those choices – our Primary Love Relationship. Whether or not a relationship turns into a marriage and that marriage does or does not last forever, the significance of a partner with whom you face life, make major decisions and share your body and home should be considered with much more gravity than we give it. Whether you're in your 20s, seeking love and partnership but not sure if you're ready for *the one*, or you're divorced and ready to draw in a kind of love you never thought possible, the formula is the same. What makes love last is: a feeling of being able to be your authentic self; the knowledge that your partner has your back and wants you to be all you can be; and – yes – a passion for each other that you learn to nurture like a garden, so that it continues to flourish and grow. Yes, it's possible! That formula is here in this book.

I'm really excited to share this information with you and, therefore, I'm not going to torture you with the long version of my life's work and life story. I've read enough self-help books to know that you just want me to get to the point. So, let's think of this more like a workbook and get right into it, shall we?

Is this for you?

First, let's make sure you're in the right place. This book is for single women who want to find a healthy, loving, committed relationship. If you are male, poly, lesbian or bisexual, feel free to read on. You may find the chapter on *The Dance* isn't written for your perspective, but you might find some gems in there anyway. Although written from a hetero-female point of view, this is ultimately about finding a healthy life partnership regardless of orientation or gender expression.

If you're ready for a grown-up, meaningful, *real deal* kind of love, this book is for you. Throughout this process you will learn how to start attracting a variety of quality men, even if you're convinced there are no good single ones out there. You're going to learn how to confidently navigate those first three months of an unformed, non-committed relationship (that awkward time where you're not sure where you stand) and you're going to find out when to cut your losses with someone sooner rather than later with your head held high.

You're also going to learn how to communicate with men so that you're speaking the same language, which can help you in every area of your life. You're going to discover a totally different way of looking at this thing we call *dating*. My promise to you is that, by the end of this book, you'll have a step-by-step strategy to start dating high-quality humans and ultimately start attracting the kind of loving partner you truly desire.

What this book is not

This is not a "text these words and get your ex back" book, or a "play hard to get and he'll chase you forever" quick-fix advice thing. This is not for man hating or man blaming. I believe that there are a lot of beautiful men out there – beautiful inside and out – and they deserve big love just like you do. This is about getting you guys to find each other!

It's important to say that neither my results nor my clients are typical. The people you're going to hear about are dedicated to their own growth and are willing to look at their part in creating their dating and relationship experience. They do the work, they check in, they're honest with themselves and they've earned their awesome partnerships. So, as with anything in life, your success is up to you.

Does this sound like you?

• Are you burning four-six months at a time with guys you probably knew were not right for you after two weeks?

• Do you secretly wonder if you're too picky and if you should just settle for living in what I like to call the *Black Hole of Mediocrity*? That's the level of attraction that's kind of *"meh,"* where you just keep hoping it will turn into more.

• Do you feel like you have to play small or dumb for men to be comfortable around you?

• Do you wake up some days and say, "I would rather be single forever than do this?" But then are you dying to have somebody to give your love and your sexiness to who's more than a friend with benefits?

• Do you ache inside when you see enviable, affectionate couples?

• Do you sometimes want to throw your cell phone across the room because you feel like men and women actually speak a different language?

• Finally, do you worry or wonder if maybe love is just not in the cards for you?

If any of these sound like you, I have some good news. None of those things are the real problem. Those are just the symptoms.

The real problem

The real problem is that you're using what I call a *default dating* approach instead of an *intentional dating* approach. Default dating is what we see every day.

Let me qualify from this point forward that when I say, "women do this" and, "men do this," I'm talking about fairly predictable generalizations. I understand that every person is unique. Try to receive the information from a non-defensive standpoint and learn what you can. In all my years of talking to women and men about relationships, I've learned that there are definitely patterns.

With that said, *default dating* is when women tend to stay

together with whoever chooses them. If a decent guy asks you out, and they've checked off a few boxes, so to speak (job, car, doesn't smell) the goal becomes to *make it work*. This leads to tolerating things, even if they don't feel good. There's a difference between giving somebody the benefit of the doubt and not honoring what you truly desire when it becomes clear you're not going to get it – which I contend becomes obvious sooner than we care to admit.

If you're having trouble believing there's anyone out there for you because you keep meeting guys who are not a good match and letting *that* sample of men determine what you believe is available, then it would be fair to say that your sample is pretty limited, yes? If you think default dating is all you have to work with, I want you to think logically about how trying to *make this relationship work* actually confirms this: you believe the other person gets to be the chooser and, therefore, gets to be intentional about who he wants to date. Somewhere in there, you may have decided that men are scarce and therefore you're going to *make it work* by default.

On the other hand, to date (and live) intentionally simply requires that you are operating from a place of *clarity in your desires* and a *belief that you can have them.* This is simple, not easy. It does require a certain amount of discipline and, as we go through this process together, you will be given tools and exercises to help you internalize a new way of approaching your relationships. It's more than just "positive thinking." We must uncover your limiting beliefs and blocks around finding a healthy life partnership and get you crystal clear about *what it is you want to be intentional about!*

Once you start using an intentional dating approach, you will suddenly feel like more interesting quality men are coming out of the woodwork. You'll be wondering where they all came from!

- You will have choices.

- You will know how to text and communicate so that you can confidently figure out if this guy is into you enough to be your king.

- You will feel desired and pursued by men who actually have relationship potential. You'll have fun romantic evenings and weekend getaways to look forward to.

- You'll wake up to texts that say, "Good morning, beautiful!"

- Ultimately, you will find someone who loves you to the bone, has your back and lets you be you – your whole you. You will finally get the chance to be that enviable, affectionate couple everyone knows is going to go home and have hot sex . . . if you like that sort of thing.

A brief introduction

Now that you know you're in the right place, I can give you a brief introduction to me and my work.

I am an author and certified life coach with a Master's in Marriage and Family Therapy. I am also the mother of two teenage girls and I've been working with women in career goals, parenting, communication and relationships for over 15 years. I specialize in empowering successful women to know their worth and find healthy, loving, sexy relationships. It is my highest mission to influence with whom women choose to have children, share a home and co-mingle their finances. Your primary love relationship is one of the most important of your life. It affects everything in your world, every day of your life. That's why this is the most gratifying thing that I do and why I'm focusing on relationships in this way.

My girls are my 24/7 life coaching clients. They keep me on my toes. I'm not married to their dad anymore, but he is a really good human. I'm glad we had our kids together and we have an exceptional co-parenting relationship at this point. I did a few things right when I was dating in my 20s and that's when I found him. Today, I am going on 11 years with my love, Mark. Finding him is a big part of why I'm inspired to do this work, so I will tell you how I discovered and put together this *Intentional Dating* approach.

My whole life with my friends, family and eventually my clients, I've been the go-to person for relationships, even though I've coached in a lot of different areas. Whenever I meet happy couples, I essentially interview them about what makes their relationship great and how they knew their partner was the one. It's my personal unofficial research project! I also feel that, for a 25-year-old child of divorce with little or no good marriages modeled for me, I did pretty well in choosing my husband. As I mentioned, we grew out of that relationship for a variety of reasons and, 12 years ago, there I was – divorced and dating again.

At 38 years old, I was aware that I had a history of choosing pretty good guys, but I also knew that I had to learn more in order to attract a love that *truly met me emotionally, spiritually and physically*, so I hired a coach. With her guiding me, I gained a level of knowledge about men, how they think and how they process information. I had to practice applying this knowledge while staying centered and true to what I wanted. That is, ultimately, how I drew in the love of my life.

Over time, in working with my clients and talking to colleagues, I've taken lots of notes . . . a book's worth! I've always had a thirst and desire to understand relationships and how men and women can really meet each other emotionally and physically. What I started to realize is that there is a big difference between those who try to *make it work* with whoever chooses them and those who intentionally seek out the real deal. I got so excited about seeing this process form up with my clients that I spent two years distilling that process into a curriculum. Now I have a way to systematically lead women to date from their authenticity and draw in a real deal love that includes deep intimacy, emotional safety and a lot of fun! This book is that curriculum.

How this book works

There are five key steps to understand and apply in order to start attracting the kind of men you want and to know you're choosing the kind of love that supports and celebrates you *in all of your awesomeness*. There will be no more playing small for anyone!

First, we will go over all five of these steps: what they are, why they matter and what it looks like to apply them, which will give you an overview.

Then I will walk you through the *how* of the process I use with my clients. This will include exercises and some basic psychological concepts. I recommend you download and print all the PDFs from my website sophievenable.com and keep them in a folder. Look at them only as you need them or you may get overwhelmed. In the chapter *The List*, you're going to create a vision statement based on a list of qualities you're seeking, but there will be more to learn. Don't do it until we get there and don't worry, we are going to circle back to that list again. It is a living document and will be amended as you grow.

It looks something like this:

The five-step overview

1. Know yourself

2. Uncover how you want to feel in a relationship

3. Learn the secret language of men

4. Dance the dance

5. Get some guidance

What follows is that guidance. This consists of the information and exercises that encompass the first four concepts in a way you can work through, step by step.

For coaching and support, visit sophievenable.com.

The Five-Step Overview

• • • • • •

You don't have to love yourself first!

Step One towards finding a real deal relationship is to *know yourself*. That sounds like a very simple concept, but what I'm trying to challenge is the notion that you have to love yourself before you find love. Let's agree to say *know yourself* instead of *love yourself* because you don't have to fall in love with yourself to find love! I know that's the opposite of all the self-help and spiritual teachings, as well as every meme you've ever seen on Facebook, but that message tends to indicate that you must have everything together and like everything about yourself before you can draw in someone who is a good match for you. That's a tall order! I see your love relationships and your friendships and your family relationships as a part of your self-love journey, not the end result or reward for it. It's healthier and more realistic to be looking for a relationship in which you can continue to grow and be a part of each other's self-love journey.

If you want to test this, just ask any happily married couple, "Did you love yourself before you met each other?" Just look at the dumbfounded looks on their faces. Some might even say to you, "No – and I still don't love myself." But what most of them will say when they understand the question is, "Not fully, but I knew I liked how she made me feel," or, "Over time she's helped me be more forgiving of my faults and my weaknesses and I've learned how to be less selfish and more patient with my partner," or she'll say, "No, I've always been really hard on my body or my intelligence, but he's taught me to be nicer to myself and more accepting of myself because he's so loving." As you can see, they're a part of each other's journey to self-acceptance. Does that make sense? Because dating is like getting a PhD in Yourself and Who You Really Are and What You Really Want.

To say that you're putting up with crappy relationships because you don't love yourself enough is not necessarily fair. You might think you're awesome in a multitude of ways, which I hope you do, but not really recognize what feels like love to you and to have someone meet you there. We get a lot of societal messages about what relationships are supposed to look like, but not really what they are supposed to *feel* like, other than instant, romantic, love-conquers-all kinds of unrealistic examples. If this were a linear journey, we would all go to a mountaintop, meditate for two years, fall in love with ourselves and magically meet Prince Charming on the way down the hill. Not only that, but that relationship would operate perfectly, which is ridiculous – right?

Know yourself

You can love yourself and be at peace with who you are, but that's not the whole picture.

You need to know your true self and uncover your old stories and limiting beliefs in order to transform how you relate with men and, therefore, *honor yourself* in the process.

Let me give you an example of my 32-year-old client. She was, and is, very successful in her own business and she felt really good about her life in most areas. However, she felt somewhat hopeless with regards to men because every guy she started to date was a project: from chronic unemployment to being an alcoholic, they were just really broken in some way. She already knew she was worthy of more than this, so she wasn't sticking around too long in these situations, but she didn't know how to change what she was attracting and experiencing.

What we discovered together was that she had some very deep-seated beliefs, not only around what it meant for her to be a woman who was single in her 30s, but also what her actual role in a relationship was supposed to be. This is because of what was modeled for her. All of the women in her family basically played nursemaid to their partners; caretaking, fixing and enabling. So even though she knew she was worthy of more than that, there became an unconscious assumption that if you want to be in a relationship, that's pretty much the deal. That's what it's going to look like to be with a life partner. She couldn't imagine any other possibilities until she acknowledged that habit of thought.

In other words, we were able to harness her positive self-esteem by acknowledging and challenging her old stories and how they didn't match up to her positive view of herself. Based on that new awareness, she was able to believe that what she wanted to experience was possible. We changed that old story and the unconscious energy around it into a new, intentional, conscious energy used to create a new story.

Now she's actually experiencing a relationship where she's supportive of him, of course – that's her nature as a giving person

– but he takes care of her as well. He makes her lunch, brings it to her at work, he cleans up the kitchen so it's all done before she gets home and other little things that really support her after a long day. She feels *partnered*. Much to her delight, she's learning to receive love at the level at which she knew she was worthy.

When you start dating from a place of authenticity and honoring what you really want, instead of attracting your old story around love by default, you begin attracting people who are more in line with what feels like love to you now as a conscious grown-up.

It's more important to *know yourself* and your limiting beliefs than it is to love everything about yourself. The beautiful, and somewhat ironic, thing is this: as you are honest with yourself and get to know your limiting beliefs, you can actually acknowledge them and accept them in a loving way – towards yourself. So, this is ultimately a process of self-acceptance and self-love that is going to uplevel the kind of partner you draw into your life.

Uncover how you want to feel

That brings us naturally to Step Two of finding a real deal relationship, and that is to uncover how you want to *feel* in a relationship. It's not about what you want in your logical mind, such as what society tells us it's supposed to look like from the outside. If you believe getting a good guy who's tall, has a job and is educated *should* make you happy, then you'll put up with however you feel in the relationship to keep trying to make it work. You do this because you've got certain things checked off and you're thinking *this is as good as it gets*.

This means that a two-dimensional vision board is not going to get you the man you want. How he looks, what kind of hobbies he has or what kind of car he drives – these facts are not going to get you on the vibration of attracting the guy who celebrates your badass in the boardroom self, who cheers you on at your half marathon and who makes you feel like his queen goddess in the bedroom.

If you've ever studied the Law of Attraction or *The Secret*, you know that it's not about wanting the car. It's about *feeling* what it will be like to have and drive the car. But this isn't just about getting the guy: this is about *assessing* the guy, because you have to get to know who he is *in a relationship*. When you know how you want to *feel in a relationship*, you don't have to waste seven months figuring out if his so-called qualifications actually make him a good partner for you. You learn to trust how you feel in your bones. Does that make sense? Because . . .

NICE IS BASELINE, PEOPLE!!

A nice guy with a job: that should be baseline. That's not *automatic relationship material*; that's just, "Hey, you get a second date!"

This part of the process is a primary section of the work we'll do in becoming intentional about your dating, so I like to frame it in a way that makes sure we're hitting all points.

I teach my clients something called a Triple-A Relationship. The three As are: Authenticity, Allegiance and Ahhh. We will go over this in greater detail in future chapters. It's based on authenticity: a feeling of knowing that you can be your whole self; allegiance: knowing that somebody has your back and cares about your growth; and Ahhh: a feeling of passion *for* this person and *from* this person. From this basic structure, we can get crystal clear on how you want to feel in a relationship and that's the best thing you can possibly do as far as getting more intentional about what you attract into your world.

Let's take that Triple-A Relationship and see how it looks.

My 26-year-old client was dating a man for almost a year. He was 34, so quite a bit older than her, had more life experience and she respected that. The Ahhh part of their relationship – the passion part – was good from the beginning, which is probably why she stayed as long as she did. However, the Allegiance part and the Authenticity part were more interesting. He seemed on one hand to be on her side because he would talk to her quite a bit about her career, but he was actually encouraging her to do things more in the way he wanted her to. He even sometimes suggested a totally different job than what she had gone to school for. She had a Master's degree and, because of that, he would give her a little crap about her school loans! Here she was: 26 years old with a completed Master's degree and she had school loans. This is not exactly shocking, but he was being critical about it.

As her coach, this drove me nuts, but it wasn't enough for her to call it quits or to really recognize what was going on in this relationship. There were other issues too, but we had discovered that she had her own fears around money and debt, so she could rationalize his criticism and make it OK. This part of the *knowing yourself* process helped, but she was not really getting the whole *on your side* thing. She could see it, but she was rationalizing it so that she didn't have to *feel* it and honor it.

But something happened around the Authenticity piece of the process that I think many women can relate to. This was very powerful for her, because one of the things she values in herself is her enthusiasm for life and her playfulness – this has nothing to do with her being young. This is just how she is and nobody's going to take that away from her! One morning, they were on a trip visiting his family and it began to snow. She ran downstairs, bouncing with excitement and squealing with delight because it was the *first time she had ever seen snow fall!* She felt so happy and goofy. She looked at his face and he wasn't smiling. Even worse, he later told her, "You know, you kind of embarrassed me with all that." She was crushed. She felt like she was being scolded for being happy. That one sentence was literally the beginning of the end for her. She called me and she was so upset. She felt like she was overreacting at the time, but, once we explored how that made her feel about being her whole self, she was really able to connect the dots about how this person wasn't on her side and wasn't capable of letting her be her authentic self. They were broken up within a month and it really stemmed from the moment that made her have to honor her need to feel safe being joyful and enthusiastic about life . . . because that is at the core of who she is.

The great news is that six months later she was dating a man who totally delights in her big energy and her enthusiasm for life. She called me about six weeks into their courtship to tell me that they'd been kayaking and she saw dolphins. A whole bunch of dolphins came swimming right next to them and she was giggling and laughing and so excited. She turned around to see this man with the biggest smile and most adoring look on his face. He was so happy for her joy and that was how she wanted to feel. Her decision to *honor how she needed to feel in a relationship* quickly brought someone into her world who could celebrate her authentic joy and enthusiasm for life.

Whether it's about seeing snow fall for the first time or what you want in the bedroom or your career, the most important thing you can do is to get in touch with how you want to feel in a relationship. The Triple-A formula will help you get specific.

The secret language of men

This brings us to Step Three, which is learning the secret language of men, and this is huge. I don't like to draw great opposing distinctions between men and women. I don't really believe that they're from Mars and we're from Venus. We're both from Earth and – believe it or not – men and women have the exact same set of emotions: happy, sad, mad, insecure, afraid, etc. Even though you might be saying, "Yeah, of course we do," you might have had a moment where you thought, "Really? We do?" This is because the range of *expressing* those emotions is so different for men than it is for women. In our culture, men can show anger for anger, but also show anger for fear and for sadness. They aren't allowed to show fear and sadness readily, so they are trained to show anger instead. Oftentimes, women will shed tears for when they are mad, sad, scared and even joyful. This really confuses men and makes them want to fix things, which can, in turn, feel disregarding to us. If we can have some compassion for each other, in recognizing that there is a societal component, we can acknowledge these differences without judgment and be able to communicate what we are actually expressing. We need to make it safer for men to express a variety of emotions other than anger. Nobody wants to date grumpy bear, so it's important to see how someone behaves over time. This is discussed in more detail in *The Onion* lesson.

When you're dating, getting to know someone involves getting them to open up a little bit, right? Let's say you've been dating for three or four weeks and you've gotten to know what I call the *outside* layer. This is who and how much they show you in the beginning. If, at this stage, you're sleeping with him, you start to think that you know this innermost layer. However, what's in the middle here, in this handy dandy little onion diagram, are two more really important layers of relating.

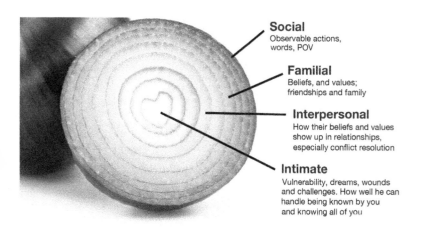

Social
Observable actions,
words, POV

Familial
Beliefs, and values;
friendships and family

Interpersonal
How their beliefs and values
show up in relationships,
especially conflict resolution

Intimate
Vulnerability, dreams, wounds
and challenges. How well he can
handle being known by you
and knowing all of you

This is how you know who he really is *in relationship*, and it takes a little experience of this person over time to get to know this. Just by choosing different words, you can actually get men to express their feelings more clearly. For example, if you ask a guy, "How do you feel about your best friend getting married," his knee-jerk response is probably going to be, "I don't know, what do you mean? It's cool, I guess." But if, instead, you ask what I like to call a *thinking question*, something like, "So, in a perfect world, when would your friend have gotten married?" that's going to get him saying things like, "Well, I actually kind of thought we would both graduate first and then maybe go to Europe together, but you know ..." This gets him in his imagination and telling you a story, which will ultimately get him more in his body about it and he'll start to naturally reveal his feelings about the situation. For example, he'll talk about how he thought they were going to go to Europe and that it is kind of a bummer because he always saw them doing this or that. Ultimately, it is the same question, looking for the same information, but it's simply a different *access point* than asking him to think about how he feels.

You've also probably at some point in your life found yourself confused by how your boyfriend or your dad or your brother came to a certain decision, specifically, how they went about processing information. Really understanding the differences between men and women in this way can help tremendously in your ability to communicate with men, to get to know them more fully and to understand their actions better.

Simply put: men are visceral. This means they process information through their bodies. They have to feel it. Women tend to be more visual. You don't really hear that very often because we're always told how men are visually stimulated sexually, but that's not what this is about. This is about how we process information. We, as women, tend to see the whole movie ahead of us. Again, these are generalizations, but the simplest example I can give you is when I had a client who was dating a guy who lived over 100 miles away, between LA and San Diego.

It's not impossible to date at this distance, but by the *third* date she was already wondering how they were going to handle seeing both families at the holidays – and all he knows at this point is that he would really like to have sex with her! He hasn't made any decision as to whether or not she's good relationship material or if they'll even still be seeing each other in December because he hasn't felt, *in his bones*, what it's like to be in a relationship with her. It's only been three dates! There is actually a lot of wisdom in that for women to learn from.

Even if he says, "Oh, we should go to Bali next summer!" or starts talking about some vacation home his family has, that just means he feels so good around you right now that this sounds fun. That doesn't mean he's actually figured out a plan or that he's even thought about the time in between. He just knows he likes how he feels around you right now. This is a really important point when it comes to navigating those first few months of the relationship. What can happen is you can hang out with a guy even though you're not that into him and continue to get attached to him because he keeps talking about going camping or skiing, or going to his parents' cabin in Aspen!

I watched a really dear friend of mine do this with a guy who was so boring and who frustrated her so much with his flakiness and unavailability. She hung with him for four months and got really emotionally attached. When they were together, when he would *finally* follow through on plans, he would start talking about going skiing up at his parents' cabin or how she would really like this beach or that beach. This made it seem like he was really *in* the relationship and, because of her default dating style, because he seemed *in*, she stayed more *in* and continued to get attached to him even though she found him incredibly boring and could not stand his communication style! The only things he talked about were what he ate and what he lifted. But, he was attractive, she was sleeping with him and she was getting more and more attached. We will talk more about this kind of attachment in the chapter on *Your Dating Perspective.*

So, even if he's talking about a future, don't default into sticking around even though you're not happy with who he is and how he's treating you. Future-talk or not, he needs to be showing you in other ways that he's a good match for you.

Understanding this concept of how men and women communicate differently is going to allow you to get to know him better. It will also mean you'll be able to talk about plans in a way that doesn't freak him out about the future or handle a conflict in a way that doesn't kill a romantic evening. The secret language of men, the expression of their emotions and their visceral processing of information: this is really powerful stuff and crucial to understand.

Let's do a quick recap. This is the work we're doing together in this book. You'll get to know your authentic self, your old beliefs, your old stories and get clear on not just the tangible qualities that you want, but how you want to *feel* in a relationship. You will come to understand how men and women think differently and how to communicate to get the most information and intimacy. Let's look at how you can do all of this and enjoy the process so you're not going bananas. That has a lot to do with Step Four, which is *The Dance.*

The dance

It's not a game, it's a dance! I now invite you to look at dating differently because appealing to a man's primitive chemistry and understanding the chase, which is really just a piece of it, is not a game. It's a dance. And the old way of teaching this stuff, like playing hard to get or withholding sex or punishing them by pouting, none of that works in the long run. It certainly doesn't move you towards true intimacy. If it's a game, there's a winner and a loser. When it's a dance, there's a leader and a follower, and, in general, men like to lead because the chase is fueled by desire and desire is a visceral experience. So when they desire you, it inspires action, right? This visceral experience of desire and action is a way to see that he's *feeling into* the relationship. If you're texting first all of the time, then you're leading. Maybe you've quickly assumed the role of girlfriend and you're starting to do his laundry by week two, hoping that he will see what a great partner you are, but what you're doing in that moment, actually, is leading the emotional depth of the relationship. You've already told him the end of the story, "Aren't I a great life partner?" Now he doesn't have any inspired action . . . and you're ghosted.

Following is not weak

It's important to remember that following is not weak. Think of ballroom dancers. She is graceful and powerful in her own right and he is leading and showing her off with grace and pride. That's a win-win. When you understand the dance, you're operating with confidence because you understand why he hasn't texted or if he's really into you enough. In fact, you waste less time and energy in those early weeks wondering because if he's not leading then you're off doing whatever makes you happy and probably getting asked to dance by other men. When you understand how men come around from courtship to commitment, you never feel like you're being a bitch when you're unavailable. You're just doing your life and that's your only job. You can be kind and you can be encouraging while still honoring your desires and taking care of your goals . . . and you don't have to lead.

Dating can be so emotional. It can be such a nerve-wracking process because waiting two days for a text feels like a week! It's important, while you're living through this, to know your priorities, to take care of them and to stay on track with your life. This is ultimately what helps you *be the real deal to attract the real deal* because there's nothing sexier than having an interesting life and not waiting by the phone.

I have to use myself as a case study here because I'm really my own best example. I had no idea how much I needed to learn about men. When I got divorced, I had a pretty good sense of self. It took me a couple of months to get my bearings and feel attractive and clear about what I had to offer to the world. I hadn't dated in a long time and I was, by nature, a very accommodating person, and I thought that was a great quality in a girlfriend! As it turns out, in dating and even, to a certain degree, in marriage, not only was it detrimental to myself but it *wasn't sexy.* My coach had to keep steering me towards taking care of myself and my goals and not letting this whole dating thing take over my psyche! Not only was I not getting things done, but I was *turning off* the guys I would meet with my accommodating, available nature.

It's just chemistry; it can't be helped. Particularly early on, they need to feel desire and you can't desire what you're already holding in the palm of your hand! I eventually mastered the *Art of Doing my Life* without feeling bad about it and I've got a thousand examples of how I kept my man all over me and continually pursuing me. Even now, this includes everything from letting him open my door – which is not because I'm helpless, but because it's a fun way to flirt – to letting him do his life without me constantly texting him. It's a forever skill that I still practice and it keeps my relationship hot. Remember: *romance* is what makes this relationship different and unique from all other relationships in your life. And romance is not a game with a winner and loser. It's a dance with a lead and follow, both of which are equally important.

Get some guidance

This brings us to Step Five: get some guidance. Intentional dating is a learnable, coachable skill. Think of it this way: if you see a therapist every week, she might help you get to the root of your weight issues, but when you're ready for actual change, she'll encourage you to hire a trainer at the gym or a dietitian. A dating and relationship coach is that person, like the trainer at the gym, who's going to teach you some skills, keep you accountable as you work towards your dreams and help you actually navigate the dating process.

This book is like a pocket coach and my approach can be simplified this way: honor self, honor other and honor the process.

We *honor self* by finding your blocks and limiting beliefs and by getting crystal clear on how you want to feel in a relationship. This is what is going to fundamentally change the kind of man that you attract into your experience.

We *honor other* by learning how men and women think and process information differently and by learning what it means to get to know someone in layers. This is how you will become an expert in deciding whether or not it is worth investing your time in this person.

Finally, *we honor the process* with everything from working on your dating profile (if you want to date online) to going on dates and practicing The Dance. Learning how Triple-A Relationships inspire long-term commitment will help you know what to be intentional about as you're getting to know each other, and help you let your relationship develop organically, according to your unique desires.

Your unique process is what's key here. So let's get started with the work!

You can absolutely do this work on your own, but if you find you want guidance or private coaching, visit sophievenable.com.

Your Single Perspective

● ● ● ● ● ●

The first thing we're going to do is look at your perspective of being single. This means your point of view (POV) of what it means to be single, where those ideas came from and how we can adjust them to keep you in a positive headspace and, therefore, enjoy the process. So, by the end of this chapter you are not only going to have a more positive perspective of being single, you are also going to have a really clear idea of what it means to *do you*, meaning what does it look like when you are *doing your life full out?* Remember, autonomy is sexy, and you want to live your day-to-day life in a way that makes you feel more confident.

This is going to benefit you for two reasons. One: it's more fun to be on a date with somebody who feels good about being single rather than somebody who is jaded. Two: somebody who is busy and involved in their own life is much more interesting and alluring than somebody who is waiting for life to happen and dependent on somebody else coming in and filling in space for them.

I'm guessing most of you are probably busier and more interesting than you realize, and I would like to help you embrace that and be aware of it. I cannot express enough how important it is to have a positive view of yourself as a single person, because it really gets you clear on what it is you bring to the table.

As you go through this process, you are not only going to have more confidence, you are going to have more clarity about your life and *what would complement your life.* This gives you a better ability to distinguish who is a good potential partner for you and who isn't. That, in turn, is going to help you waste less time, which is the tortuous part of this dating thing, right? We always feel like we are burning time, and that's what I want to help you avoid. Of course, it's important to acknowledge that this process does take time (all good things do) and that it's never really wasted. If you can approach it in a way that is efficient and positive then you will ultimately feel like it's not wasted time and that you are always learning.

I'm not asking you to fall in love with being single or even fall in love with yourself. I'm not asking you to fall in love with yourself before you find love. Being in a loving relationship is part of the growth process that helps you, over your lifetime, achieve the elusive feeling of self-love. That's what I want for you.

So, instead of asking you to fall in love with yourself, I am asking you to *get to know yourself* and to appreciate your life as an individual.

We are going to do two things:

1. Learn a concept called Reframing.

2. Look at six areas of your life, prioritize them according to your desires and give you little goals within those areas so you can feel good in the day to day.

Reframing

Reframing is defined as a way of viewing and experiencing events, ideas and emotions to find more positive alternatives. Some people might see this as silver lining thinking, but it's a little bit different than that.

Let's look at what it's not. Reframing is not denial. It's not, "Oh, he broke up with me." Reframe: "No he didn't, I broke up with him." It's also not, "Well, he broke up with me, so the silver lining is that I don't have to go to that wedding and I can go on that trip with my sister." That's closer, but a true reframe would be: "He broke up with me." Reframe: "We weren't the match that I deserve and he let me go so that I could find something better." You see how the *internalized meaning* is changed, not just the circumstantial result?

Reframing is an important skill because, as we go through life, things are not always going to go as expected. You might lose a job, you might lose a relationship or bang up your car and those things not only affect our experience, but they affect our perception of ourselves. *They literally affect our self-worth and how we feel about ourselves.* That's why the difference between the silver lining thinking is important. Silver lining is more situational and is just looking at some luckier aspect of the outcome, whereas a reframe is with regards to how the circumstance is internalized and affects your view of yourself in the situation. That's going to be a much deeper, much more meaningful reframe.

Think of reframing things that happen to you as a way of keeping you in a frame of mind that the *universe is on your side* and that your life is not some sort of cosmic mistake! Avoid claiming that everything that happens to you keeps happening to you for all the worst reasons. Instead, find the lesson in the things that happen and be gentle with yourself as you would a young child.

Reframing Being Single

check · challenge · change

1	who:	when:	negative pov:	positive pov:

2	who:	when:	negative pov:	positive pov:

3	who:	when:	negative pov:	positive pov:

The process of reframing has three parts to it: **Check**, **Challenge** and **Change**. You can look at the sample worksheet and / or print out the PDF called "Reframing Being Single" at <u>sophievenable.com</u>

When I say "**check**" I mean *check in with the feeling* so that you can name the negative statement or point of view (POV). The first two things on the left of the PDF are: who and when. What this means is *when did you hear this perspective of being single and who said it?* Was it your grandma your entire life growing up, or maybe your mom repeated, "If you don't get married by the time you are 22, you are going to be an old maid." This would give you a negative point of view such as *I'm running out of time* or *I'm getting too old to attract a man.* The fear around that is what we are checking in with so that you can name what you've been taught or what you've been telling yourself. So, in this old maid example, even if you know that, in this day and age, you can definitely be married later than 22, it may still have been repeated so many times to you as a child that on some level you believe it. Again, that's what you want to **check** in with: *When I'm feeling negative or heavy or scared, what is the negative point of view?*

Now that you are aware of the negative point of view, we **challenge** it by simply asking if it's really true? Bring that belief system into your conscious thought process and hold it up against your current reality. No, of course it's not true!

So we **change** it. You may change it to *I'm taking my time choosing the right life partner or my confidence from being older and wiser is what makes me more attractive and sexy to the right man.*

What if a good girlfriend of yours keeps saying, "Being single is awesome, and looking for a relationship is stupid," and part of you believes that, but it feels like a negative point of view for you? I suppose it could also be a positive point of view, but if you are reading this book I am assuming this statement might be a negative because you have a desire to attract a healthy relationship. So, if you **check** in with it and it feels like a negative point of view, then you **challenge** it.

You **challenge** that point of view by asking *is it true for me?* You can go further and ask *is there any good I can take from that?* And *what is it that I want from this exact point forward?*

These questions can help you come up with your reframe:

- Is it true?

- Is there any nugget of goodness in it?

- What do I want?

In this example you could reframe her statement into, "Yes, there are things to enjoy right now about being single and taking care of my life, but I know that consciously choosing how I want to attract the right partner is empowering and healthy for me."

Let's take a non-dating example like, "I got into a stupid accident and totaled my car. My life is such a mess." The challenge would be:

- Is it true?

"Yeah, I did. I totaled my car. But, it wasn't the worst accident because I am here and alive and talking about it. It also doesn't mean my whole life is a mess, it just means that I got in an accident today and that is a bummer."

• Is there any good that can come from it?

"Well, I realized I need to slow down. I'm alive to tell it, so that's good."

Then, the third question,

• What do I want now?

"Well, I want a car with a nicer interior and better handling."

So the reframe would be:

"I feel lucky to have walked away from an accident today. I'm going to slow down a bit in life and now I get to shop for a new car."

Again, gentle, like you would be with a child. Nothing to the effect of, "I'm not going to be so stupid and rush around like a crazy woman!" The nugget of goodness is that you got a cheap lesson to slow down and appreciate your life. Reframe it to help your view of the situation *and* your view of yourself.

Work with the PDF and see if you can come up with three things to reframe. Think about any negative feelings or fears you have around being single and where and when you learned them. It can even be from yourself! You could be the one saying the negative thing your whole life or perhaps since a breakup or a divorce. **Check** it out, see if you can **challenge** it with those questions and then **change** it for the better.

You do you

The next thing we are going to do to improve your single perspective is focus on your day-to-day life. We are going to look at six areas of your life and prioritize them. This is going to help you see how full your life is with or without a partner and figure out if there are any areas that need tending to regardless of whether you are single or not. Relationships work best when two whole people with full lives come together and complement each other. Sometimes people can lose their own identity in a relationship and start to build their life around the other person. This is something we've all seen, either in our friends or in ourselves.

I'm not talking about, "Oh, my fiancé is in the military. I've got to move to Virginia." Well, of course you do. That's fine. What I am talking about is when women stop hanging out with their friends or pursuing their hobbies. They stop taking care of themselves physically sometimes. I know it's a little more fun to stay in bed and cuddle than go to yoga class, but you need to continue your self-care and this needs to be established from the beginning. You want to make sure you are taking care of your life and taking care of your priorities from the get-go. This is for two reasons. One: your new partner can see how awesome you are. Two: they understand what your passions and priorities are and they can support them.

It's not fair to not take care of your life and then get mad at them later because you are not taking care of your life. That's on you. You need to come into the situation saying, "This is how my life works. These are my priorities; these are the things I love to take care of; this is what I am passionate about." When you do this, you will have clarity and confidence; your partner will have the things they are passionate about and taking care of in their life; and the two of you can support each other because your lives complement each other. That is the ideal situation. What we are going to focus on now is this chart that has the six areas of your life sectioned out. Those areas are: work, health, family, friends, quiet time and, of course, dating. You can download and print these PDFs at sophievenable.com.

My Personal Priorities

order 1-6

☐ work: _____

☐ health/fitness: _____

☐ family: _____

☐ friends: _____

☐ date nights: _____

☐ quiet time: _____

Look at the categories. If you want to scratch one of them out and change it, that's fine. If you even want to print out a second PDF and add a couple of categories, that's also fine. I really want this to work for you. Use the little boxes on the left to prioritize these categories one through six, with one representing the number one thing that's important to you right now. This can be for right now, this week or this month. For example, maybe you are working towards a promotion at work and that is your top priority.

Your priorities will ebb and flow and maybe even switch from week to week or month to month. Nobody else is going to look at this, so if work is priority over family *for a minute*, that's your business. Do what feels right and authentic to you.

It's always nice to have really specific goals for each area of your life. Go through each segment and think about some potential goals. You only need to pick one or two things. We're starting with small steps, not giant milestones. Let's take work, for example. You might want to work towards a promotion or you might have goals as simple as, "I really want to be on time every day," or, "I want to make sure that on Fridays I have cleared out my inbox so that I can truly relax on the weekend." These are great goals.

Put a few little notes next to the word "work," and be clear about what it is you want to work towards in that area. Let's take health and fitness next. Do you want to make sure you are taking medicine every day for a health issue that you have? Or do you want to work out four days a week? Do you want to start going for a walk every morning? All these things are important for you and your quality of life.

With regards to your family, what would be ideal for you? Be specific. Do you want to be sure to call your mom every Sunday? Or do you want to have dinner with your family on Friday nights? What would it look like to be fulfilling this part of your life?

Let's look at the friends category. This is important because often when we get involved in a relationship, we can get swept away in the process and forget about our friends. Fortunately, with Facebook, Instagram and other social media, we can keep up with each other's lives. It still doesn't feel good to have a friend completely disappear into a relationship. We all have a certain amount of compassion for the situation in that we know it's exciting to be in a new relationship, but sometimes the disappearing act goes on too long. Now is the time to think about what it would look like if you were keeping up with your friendships. Are there any friends you really miss who you haven't caught up with in a while?

Are there phone calls you need to make or emails you need to send? Do you want to reserve Friday nights to make sure you go out with your girlfriends and not worry about meeting guys?

Dating is also one of your priorities right now. Let's think about what you really want this to look like. Would you like to have one date a week? Would you like to have two dates a month? Do you want to make sure you check your match.com emails once a day, but not 18 times a day? How would you like your dating life to ultimately look? Once again, this is for right now. This is for the next week or the next month; we're not looking at 18 months from now. These can be small goals like, "I want to let my friends know that I really am looking for something," or, "I want to call this friend and say I thought that guy at her party was cute and find out if he is single." Again, these can be small goals – a very simple picture of what you would like your dating life to look like.

Take note while you are writing about your dating life and what you want it to look like. What are you feeling in your body and where? Do you feel light or tight in your chest? Do you feel excited or annoyed? Are there any particular feelings in your body that you are noticing? Simply take note of it without judgment. This is how you find your truth in your body. This is a process I will continue to introduce to you on a basic level as we go through this book.

Quiet time can also be hobby time and it's more important to your dating life than you might think. It can be things you do for yourself like learning to play an instrument, going to a belly dancing class, quilting, knitting or reading books. This is really important time for you and it's very difficult to maintain when you first start dating somebody. Here's the thing: I'm not telling you to turn down dates *just* so that you can have your quiet time. I do, however, want you to remember what you value about your quiet time, so that if and when a date falls through or somebody turns out to be a jerk, you are not going to betray yourself and go out simply because you cannot stand the thought of being alone. You are going to say, "No, I have better things to do. I have a duck scarf to knit for my friend, and that is better than going on a lousy date."

I have included a blank calendar in the PDFs available at sophievenable.com which you are welcome to print out. What I like to do with my clients is to look at their time off. See what nights make you really uncomfortable, take a highlighter and highlight them. Perhaps you're thinking, "I always know my roommate is not home," or, "I never have anything to do on Wednesday nights. That makes me dread it and I'm so aware of feeling single." These are the nights I want you to highlight so you can compare them to your quiet time list and remind yourself that you have those options.

Sunday	Monday	Tuesday	Wednesday	Thursday	Friday	Saturday
	yoga					
	yoga		yoga		date!	
	yoga		yoga	girl's night!		
	yoga		yoga			
	yoga		yoga	girl's night!		

Now these nights are highlighted, if a date falls through you have the option to go to the gym or call a friend. When you look at your personal priorities and all the things you have going on in your life, a date not coming through isn't going to crumble your whole world. This means when you are approaching that Wednesday or Thursday night when you don't have plans, you can actually start looking forward to those nights off, because you can now catch up on a TV show or finish a book. Whatever it is, I would discourage you from filling those nights with Instagram and Facebook and looking at what everybody else is doing.

I would love for you to focus on quiet time, hobby time or personal time – something that feeds your soul. Something you do just for you. When you really look at your life, you only have so many hours you can give to yourself. Take advantage of having clarity around this topic and remember that there is this thing you really love doing that you may have forgotten about because you were so worried about dating. Look at all of this very specifically. Be intentional about it. As you are filling this out you can change it, try it and see how it feels. I invite you to take note of your feelings. If you are feeling anxious about it or resistant to doing this at all, it doesn't have to make complete sense to you. Again, be aware of your body and take note of what you are feeling.

The more you can practice noticing the feelings in your body, the more you can become aware of just how powerful your thoughts and beliefs are. Joe Dispenza, my favorite brain-scholar-extraordinaire and author of *Breaking the Habit of Being Yourself* explains it this way: your thoughts create emotion, your emotions create a mood, your moods create a temperament, your temperament over time becomes your personality and, "your personality creates your personal reality." So as you uncover and name your thoughts and beliefs around being single, notice how you are feeling in your body. We can't change what we don't acknowledge so we must acknowledge what in our current way of looking at our dating experience feels heavy and frustrating and what feels lighter and happier. Reframing helps redirect and refile those lousy feelings towards a more positive perspective. This is the first step to creating a new relationship reality.

Your Dating Perspective

• • • • • •

Now we are going to focus on your dating perspective. In the same way we were looking at creating a more positive perspective around *being single*, now we are going to focus on creating a more positive perspective of dating itself – the whole process. This process is important for two reasons. One: dating takes a lot of time and energy, so you want to use it effectively. The more time you spend going down roads that are fruitless, the more frustrated and impatient you can become with the process. That frustration starts to influence and define your whole "story" around dating. We want to tighten up the filter on the dates you accept and on the potential partners you put a lot of energy into when you might know it's not worth it in the first place. Doing your Vision Statement in the next chapter is going to be a big part of creating that filter too.

The second reason this process is important is because choosing your life partner is *one of the most important decisions you will make in your adult life.* You might be looking for a partner to marry and have children with, or maybe you are divorced and looking for a life partner who will mesh well with your kids. These are all incredibly important decisions.

Your primary love relationship affects everything. It affects your day-to-day life. It can affect where you live. It can affect your finances. It can affect your psychological well-being, so we want it to be positive. This is not a decision to be taken lightly or approached with impatience. You can rush things, get heavily invested before you know if that person is worth putting your time into and gloss over major flaws because you don't want to go back to square one. This is a process that I call "spackling" and I will refer to it many times in this book. Spackle, if you don't know, is the white paste you use to fix cracks in drywall. If you are trying to use it to fix anything of a serious nature, however, it will eventually not hold up. If you get into the habit of spackling, it can burn months, sometimes years of your life.

The other thing that can happen when you have a negative feeling about the dating process is that when you are dating with a jaded energy, you can get a skewed view of the people you are dating. You could miss a really nice guy who might have been nervous. You might accidentally put off somebody who likes you because you give off a negative vibe due to being so frustrated with the process. Truth be told, the conversation about *how crappy dating is* is really not a good dating conversation topic. People get into it all the time, but what ends up happening is one or both of you are wondering, "Are they trying to send me a subliminal message?" This makes everything awkward and negative. If you find yourself going down that path, just change the conversation and start talking about how you have really enjoyed meeting some nice people, but you are really looking for a good match. Turn it around and keep it positive in a way that says, "I have a belief that I could meet the right person."

Once you do the work in this chapter, you will have a more positive perspective of dating. You will also understand the process that tends to keep us in situations longer than we should be. Firstly, we are going to look at a fun way to assess relationships, then we are going to explore a concept called "intermittent reinforcement." This is a behavioral psychology concept that is really important to understand. After this, we are going to go back to the reframing that we did in the previous chapter. We'll apply this to the dating process and to some of your negative dating experiences. One of the things we are trying to do is to get you to have a more efficient dating experience. In other words, to not waste your time on a lot of bad dates, or waste six, eight or even 24 months in a relationship you know is not your happy place. I want to introduce you to something I use to measure relationship satisfaction. Until somebody gives me a better name for it, I am calling it the WMT graph. "WMT" stands for "Worth My Time." It's going to help you visualize where you really stand with a potential guy and whether or not you want to invest more time in him.

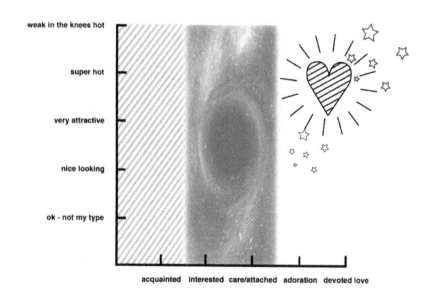

Here's our basic graph. On the left side, or the Y axis (going up and down,) we are going to look at your level of physical attraction. This starts with, "Hmm he's OK. He's not really my type," and goes to, "Yeah, he's nice looking," then on to, "Very attractive," then to, "Super hot! Not quite sure what I might do around him," and finally to, "Weak in the knees hot. Oh, my God. This could be trouble or it could be totally amazing."

On the X axis, we are going to look at your emotional investment. This starts with getting acquainted with each other, then moves into becoming interested in him. Then we come to care and attachment, which is when you really start to care about this person. You really want good things to happen for them. You really like who they are as a person. I want to clarify, however, that this is not necessarily the same as you being really happy with what you are getting from the relationship. This is just from your point of view. After time, this care and attachment moves into adoration. You simply adore this person. You really love everything about them. Naturally, over time, this moves into devoted love. This is when you not only adore them, but you really see your future with them. You feel this is your happy place and being here inspires you to be your best person because you want to be his happy place too.

Now, let's look at that gray striped area. If you are going to spend a lot of time with somebody in this area, you pretty much have a friend with benefits, or maybe just a friend. Now, the shiny, beautiful area with the hearts and stars is where you are feeling super attracted, feeling lots of adoration and are really happy. Situations like this are rarely ever a waste of time. This is the goal in what we are going for. These are really special connections – happy, happy, happy.

Where I want to direct your attention to, and what I want to focus on right now, is the area right in the middle. I like to refer to it as the Black Hole of Mediocrity. These are the dating situations and the newly unformed relationships that simply go on too long. These inspire excuses like, "Well, you don't get rid of a guy like that. I mean he's nice," or, "But, he was so excited and sweet a month ago. I think he is just stressed right now," or worse, "It's better than doing nothing." It's not better than doing nothing.

If you suspect you are in a situation like this, I want you to ask yourself one question: What would it be like if I didn't see him anymore? And if your gut reaction is, "Oh my gosh, I can't imagine not being with him. I love how I feel around him," then there might be more to explore. But, if your first reaction is, "Uh, I don't want to go back to square one," or, "But, he's nice," or, "But, I think he might be interested," that's not a reason to stick around. If he's a nice guy, he deserves to be with somebody who loves being around him, and if your response is, "But, I don't know, I mean I think he likes me," that's not enough either. This has to be because you are feeling really interested in him, and you really like who he is as a person. I can give you 1,000 reasons not to get reeled back in, but it's hard because I guarantee that the second you get out of that mediocre situation, he is going to suddenly become more attentive. It's truly the nature of things.

This attentiveness can become really addictive and can keep drawing you back in. You think, "Oh, he really does like me," but the more important thing for you to think about in that moment is, "Yeah, OK, he is calling me back, but do I really like him or do I just like that I've gotten his attention again?" You need to ask yourself, "Do I really like how I feel around him, and do I like how I feel when I'm not around him? Is he good at making me feel like we are still connected? Does he leave me with a feeling that I am special to him and that he can't wait to see me again?"

From the other point of view, as far as what you are receiving and whether or not that is part of the Black Hole of Mediocrity you are in, is how he is pursuing you. I like to say you want to see tenacity and transparency over time, and that really shows you that a guy is genuinely interested. You can really see if you like how you feel when he is behaving that way – when he is pursuing you. Are you excited? Are you happy to see him too? Tenacity is his consistent effort to see you and to be in your airspace, and transparency is his ability to be obvious about his feelings for you. He is not leaving you guessing or friend zoning you or making you never really feel like you are sure he is attracted to you. It's really obvious when a guy is into you because he compliments you and he wants to be around you. Even if he is a little shy and not great with words, he makes it very clear that he is into you.

When he does this over time is when you can tell that this guy really is interested. When I say "time," I don't mean two weeks! Anybody can be super excited, projecting all kinds of qualities onto you and be the best guy in the world for two or three weeks. However, if this suddenly dies off and he is not trying to get in touch with you and his communication sucks, you have found yourself in a mediocre situation. The reason it's addictive is because of . . . *dun da da . . . intermittent reinforcement.*

Intermittent reinforcement is a term that originates from American psychologist BF Skinner's theories on operant conditioning and behaviorism. Intermittent reinforcement is when a reward that increases a desired response is given only part of the time that a subject gives the desired response. In short, BF Skinner spent a lot of time with rats, and you don't have to understand all of the subtleties of this concept. What you do need to understand is that this is a reward schedule so powerful it's why Las Vegas, which started as a few little motels in the middle of the desert, is now a gambling megatropolis larger than Miami or New Orleans.

Yes, your basic slot machine can give you great insight into your dating experience.

Think about it this way: if you knew you were going to get a pat on the back every time you completed a task, you would complete that task but eventually get bored. However, if you knew you were going to get a pat on the back every third time you completed a task, you would keep going a little longer and probably work a little harder before that third time to make sure you were definitely going to get the reward. If − like the slot machine − you never knew when you were going to get the reward, you would continue to do the task until you were completely exhausted, or − in the case of the slot machine − until you were out of money, or, for some people, until you had lost everything.

What we know about unpredictable reinforcement is that it's extremely addictive and it truly is what Vegas is built on. But, enough about gambling − let's talk relationships. When a guy calls or texts you just enough to keep you in his back pocket − that's intermittent reinforcement at work. When he's communicating so poorly that you are totally frustrated with him, but then his text comes in and you feel happy, you have to stop and ask yourself, "Does this guy really want to see me, or is he just making sure he can still have an effect on me?" You have to look at how much of this is an addictive process for your ego. What happens is that when he's not calling, you start to feel bad about yourself, and when he actually does call you, suddenly you feel better about yourself. At this point, it's not even about him! It's about you and how you are feeling about yourself, but his attention becomes the stimulus. You are completely losing sight of whether or not you even like this guy. You are actually just starting to get caught up in a chemical addiction to the happy brain chemicals that go off when you get that text message.

Let's go back to the example of my friend who was dating the boring guy. Overall, he seemed like a really nice person who, even though his texting and communication was pretty basic for the first couple of weeks, was really attentive and always asking to make plans. Things looked good. At first, it seemed to me and her other friends that all he could talk about was working out and eating. *Maybe he's nervous*, we thought. It turned out that, no, that's really all he talks about. After a couple of weeks, his communication started to get weird. He would text her and say, "Hey, what's up? What are you doing today?" But, then he'd fall asleep and not text back, ultimately not making any plans. So, she understandably started to spin and obsess and feel really confused. I kept asking her, "Do you like this? I mean, he's a terrible communicator." And she'd say, "Well, I think that's just how he communicates." Then, *again*, the question is, "So do you like that? Do you want to have a relationship with somebody who communicates like this?" She'd say, "But he was so sweet in the first couple of weeks." And I totally get it. He was. However, very limited credit should be given for, "he was nice in the first two weeks." Nice is baseline. Remember, guys get a rush from succeeding with girls and they do like getting a response from you. They like knowing they have an effect on someone. Everybody does.

So, in her frustration, she finally pulled back. And then, of course, he started giving her more attention and asked to make plans. So, now with her head on straight, she realized that this guy has never asked her anything about her life, he has no idea what she wants in life, and – oh my God – he really does only talk about what he lifts and what he eats. She was able to see that he communicated with her just enough to keep her in his back pocket.

Ultimately, she stopped falling for it and redirected her energy towards finding somebody she was interested in, because that is the problem with this Black Hole of Mediocrity. You're actually losing sight of what you want, what makes you happy and who you actually enjoy being around. This is because you're getting intermittently reinforced by unpredictable bursts of attention from somebody who, once you're spinning, you're forgetting to look at through the eyes of, "Is this worth my time? Do I like how he's pursuing me?" And, wow, you can waste a lot of time and energy – as well as drive yourself bananas – in these situations.

Another common way this can manifest is like this: let's say you get past that first couple of months with somebody who is kind of *good enough*. So now, you're both being intermittently reinforced with a feeling of being coupled and there's probably also some sexual bonding. This situation is addictive for both of you because even though it's better than being single, it also comes with a lot of frustration and disappointment and maybe even some fighting. And you can't even really point out why you're in this situation other than momentum and sexual bonding, which is something we'll talk about more in *The Onion* chapter. The inevitable experience is that physical intimacy creates the perception of emotional intimacy. But, really, what you find yourself wishing a lot is that he is different from who he is. This is where we date for potential. Again, the reason this is so addictive is because you're being intermittently reinforced by that feeling of being coupled, of sexual bonding, of going out with your friends, drinking and having fun. But, when you come home, are you happy? Is this your happy place? And this is where I get on my soapbox. Ladies and gentlemen: there's no reason to continue a relationship that is stuck in this area. This is not an area where people and souls grow, expand and gain the benefit of being in a relationship, because being in a loving relationship should be a bonus in your life and something that helps you expand as a person. You should be literally looking for somebody to grow with. You're on this quest and you're going on these interviews to say, "Are you going to be my best friend, my best ally and are you somebody I can give my best to?" That's where this really has to come from. Are you somebody I can give my best to and are you somebody who's worthy of it? And you thought you were just looking for steady sex. (Just kidding.)

Before we move on to reframing, let's do a quick review so far. We've learned that the biggest reason we develop a negative point of view of the dating process is because we spend too much time in situations that are not worth our time. This is either by accepting dates from nice guys we're not really attracted to or allowing ourselves to remain available to guys who don't demonstrate the three "Ts" – Tenacity and Transparency over Time. We also learned that the reason we allow ourselves to stay in these crummy situations is intermittent reinforcement. So, whenever you feel yourself spinning about a guy, you're going to imagine yourself at a slot machine or, if you really want to put an end to it quickly, imagine yourself as a lab rat. In conclusion: don't be a lab rat!

So, now that you know so much and you're so darn smart, go ahead and print out your Black Hole of Mediocrity PDF and chart some of your relationships. Place your past relationships on the graph. You can even place them twice. You can say, "This is where we started and this is where we were." So, it might look like this: "Jeff beginning," "Jeff at one year together" and "Jeff end." Because sometimes they do regress. On the Y axis, there's generally some shift. Somebody can become really attractive as you start to fall more in love with them and they get sexier every day. But they can also turn out to be a jerk and get a lot less attractive. Either case can happen and it's good to be aware of that. Then, in your goal area on this graph, draw your own little hearts or stars – or whatever makes you happy – in the area where you would like to find somebody. As always, be aware of how you're feeling as you're doing this exercise.

Reframing your dating perspective

Now we're going to take reframing, which we applied to your single perspective, and we're going to apply it to dating and to your dating experiences. So, as a review, remember reframing is a way of viewing and experiencing events, ideas and emotions to find more positive alternatives. The way we reframe is to **check, challenge** and **change**, right? **Checking** means we're checking in with our feelings and naming the habitual thought (or thoughts) we may be having. We can further acknowledge where and from whom we learned that negative point of view. And then we **challenge** that thought and we use these questions: "Is it true?" "Is there anything good in the experience that I can pull out of this?" and "What do I want?" Those three questions are going to help you construct your new perspective so you can replace that negative perspective with your new positive reframe. If you look at your PDF, which you can print at sophievenable.com, you have your little reminder at the top there – **check**, **challenge**, **change**. You have room on the left to put where and with whom and when the date was. Then, of course, you have an area for your negative point of view and your newly constructed positive point of view. You may think you can skip this because you went through this process for "being single." Please don't skip it. These exercises and the process of writing them out, taking them from your brain to the paper, are an important part of truly understanding and changing your dating experience.

So, let's take a couple of quick examples. Let's say your habitual thought is, "Dating sucks" or, "All guys are jerks." The first clue to the fact that this is a habitually negative point of view is the use of *globalizing statements*. Any time you use the words "always," "never," "all" or "every time," that's a clue that you want to **check** in with that statement. Take the statement, "Dating sucks. All guys are jerks." We want to **check** in with that statement, acknowledge it as a negative point of view and then **challenge** it. So, is it true? Does dating really suck? Are all guys jerks? Or did you go on some bad dates where some guys turned out to be jerks, and have you also listened to your friends' stories and come up with this global idea that dating just sucks and it sucks for everybody? Pick out what is actually true about that statement and then ask yourself,

"Is there anything good in the experience? Did I learn anything from it? Did I have a good time? Did I meet a nice person? Did I see a good movie? Did I stretch out of my comfort zone? Or, did I wear a really cute outfit that I didn't even know I could pull off?" Acknowledge anything you can extrapolate from any of your experiences in dating.

Reframing Dates & Dating

check · challenge · change

1
who:

when:

negative pov:

positive pov:

2
who:

when:

negative pov:

positive pov:

3
who:

when:

negative pov:

positive pov:

Then ask, "What do I want now?" Of course, what we're doing in this book is talking about what you want overall for your dating experience. You want to meet quality people, you want to have a good time and you want to be fishing in a pond that's stocked with the kind of people you want to meet. So, let's reconstruct that initial "dating sucks" statement to this: "Dating is a challenging, but exciting, process that gives me the opportunity to meet my perfect match," or maybe, "Dating gives me opportunities to learn about myself and what I'm really looking for." These are ways you can reframe an idea that you might have about the dating process in general. You can also reframe dating experiences specifically. Think about this statement, "That was a really crappy date and a waste of time." Let's **check** in with that and then **challenge** it. Was it really a bad date? Was it really crappy? Yeah, maybe it was. OK. Is there any good that can come of it? Was he really not very smart and you learned that you need to be with a smart person? If so, that also answers the question, "What do I want now?" Are you thinking, "Oh, he really couldn't keep up with anything I was talking about and that was not fun." If so, you learned that you need to be with somebody who's quick-witted. Now think, "What do I want now?" An answer might be, "I want to find somebody who can keep up with me intellectually." Great. So here, the reframe is that this date taught you that you need to look for somebody who is quick-witted and who can keep up with you intellectually.

We don't even have to focus on the bad part of the date, because it's really easy to get caught up in gossiping and telling stories and laughing about how awful dating is. As humans, we love to bond over pain. It's much easier to complain and bond over negativity than it is to discuss our successes because, in our culture, this tends to be looked at as showing off or bragging. It's sort of fun and funny to continue to talk about how bad our dating experiences are or how much of a jerk every guy you go out with is. Well, you know what? Maybe this guy is just not your guy. He might be fantastic for somebody else. He might be really sweet, but can't keep up with you – and that's cool. He can keep up with somebody else and make her really happy. So, let's focus on reframing the experience into something positive: what can you take away from it? Then let go of the rest. *Do not feed that story.* Don't perpetuate the negative point of view because, remember, your life experiences affect your perception of yourself. Therefore, a negative perception of your experiences can add to a negative perception of yourself. That's why reframing is so important. You can print out one, two, three copies of this PDF. Go over some feelings about dating in general, go over some dating experiences you've had and see if you can turn those into positive experiences you can look back on and learn from. And, as always as you're doing this, be in touch with how you're feeling about it.

The List

● ● ● ● ● ●

Now we are going to get into some fun stuff! This is where I want you to get into your more visceral, storytelling side and think about, or *feel about*, how you want your real deal relationship to be.

This exercise may take some time. Be patient with it and with yourself. It will require some writing, but I will provide you with some guidance and even writing prompts so that you can complete it with confidence. Do not skip this part – it is the most important part of changing, creating and keeping your vision of your new relationship. There is no short cut.

A different kind of list

We've all got a "list" in our heads of qualities we would like in a partner. Most women say they would like a man who is nice, attractive, employed, fun, outdoorsy maybe and stable. I hear "stable" a lot. Many will say, "I want a gentleman," and, curiously, only a few will say, "He needs to be good in bed." I'm always a little concerned by how low on the priority list having sexual chemistry is for most women. I believe this stems from the societal message that, "Sex shouldn't be that important because it dies down anyway," or, "If you really love each other, sex isn't that important." These are lies that keep us from tending to our sex lives as though they matter. The third A in the Triple-A Relationship is about passion. A life partnership does not last in a happy and loving manner without a *shared level of satisfaction* around physical intimacy. That level can be whatever you both agree on, but there must be some level or you will become roommates. A life partner is someone you face life with on a familial, social, survival and sexual level. So as you are filling this out, remember that this is private and nobody has to see it. This list will help you be more specific about exactly what it means to be "stable" or "a gentleman" or "good in bed."

It may seem, as you're going through this, that you are "setting the bar too high" or "being too picky." That's what the world likes to tell you about honoring your desire. For example, the bit about how he responds when you cry . . . the man you're with might not respond the way you want him to the first time, but because you're only going to partner with someone who has your back, he would be the kind of person you could talk to about that and let him know what would be helpful. Then he would be able to respond that way for you because, by doing this exercise, you realized that you actually do have a desired response! In that way, you are literally creating the man of your dreams by creating this list.

My suggestion is that you read through the whole thing one time and get a sense of what jumps out to you. Then go through it and give thoughtful responses. Get as detailed as you like, especially when something makes you feel light and excited.

If something doesn't apply to you, feel free to skip or change it. If you are struggling with an answer, or if something makes you feel anxious or heavy, imagine a scenario and feel into how you would like to be telling someone about it later. For example, if you have a certain amount of social anxiety and even *thinking* about being at a party together makes you want to skip the question, imagine a scenario where you felt seen and taken care of and how you would like to tell a friend about it later. Instead of assuming that your anxiety is a relationship liability, imagine feeling understood and accepted *right where you are* with it and what that might look like in action. The last question, about dealbreakers, refers to those things you know you can't live with. Generally, these tend to be around religion, kids and monogamy. If you know you must marry or partner with someone of your faith, then not being in that faith, or being willing to convert, would be a dealbreaker. If you know you cannot be monogamous, and you want an alternative lifestyle, then monogamy would be a dealbreaker for you. If you want children, then someone who does not want them is probably not someone you want to spend time getting emotionally attached to.

Using your printed PDF (available at sophievenable.com,) be honest with yourself about your desires and fill in this list as if there are no limits to what you can have. Remember, dating with intention means being clear about your desires and believing you can have them. *Complete this list as though you are six-eight months into your happiest relationship* and a friend you haven't seen in a while says, "Tell me everything!" and you have the BEST news in the world for her.

After you do the list, there is one more exercise, so come back to this chapter when you are done.

External / Tangible

His look / type?

Height?

How "health conscious" or "fit" would you prefer?

Particular facial features?

Is he vegetarian, vegan, omnivore, etc?

What city does he live in?

Education level?

What kind of work?

Any kind you really don't want?

Income range?

Internal / Social / Lifestyle

Is he punctual?

Can he handle being late?

Does he like birthdays?

Anniversaries?

Is he affectionate in public?

Is he more introverted or extroverted?

Is he social and willing to go out with you?

Does he like a quiet night at home?

Does he like parties?

Does he like hosting parties?

What is his religion?

Political party?

Are politics a passion for him?

How does he feel about your best friend?

How do your family and friends feel about him?

What does your dad (brother, friend) say about him?

What does your mom (sister, friend) say about him?

Is he more of a realist or a dreamer?

What kind of relationship does he have with his family?

Does he like kids / babies?

Does he have / want kids?

Is he a dog person?

Is he a cat person?

What are his hobbies?

What's the one kind of music he doesn't like?

Does he like coffee in the morning? Tea?

What's his vacation style? Would he rather go to Yosemite to hike or Hawaii to lie around and drink umbrella drinks? Or go surfing? Or both?

Does he drink?

If so, is he happy / friendly when drinking?

Does he smoke?

Is he very sexual?

Is he sexually adventurous?

What sexual attributes would you like? (Good kisser, stamina, not too often, every day, open-minded, not too open-minded, conservative)

What about your sexuality does he accept / understand?

How He Makes You Feel

Do you feel emotionally safe with him?

Do you feel secure in his feelings for you? His commitment to you?

If he goes out with his friends, how do you feel about that?

How does he introduce you to people at parties?

Can he be independent without you?

Do you trust him?

How does he respond to your successes?

How does he give you affection in public?

Is he affectionate with you alone?

If so, what does that look like? (Back tickles, head petting, hand holding . . .)

How does he handle an argument?

How do you feel after the resolution?

If you are upset / crying what does he do to help?

Does he open the door for you?

Does he pay the check? If so, how often?

What does the relationship look like?

How often do you go on dates?

Are you together every night?

Do you go for walks or stay in and watch movies?

How often do you go out without him? (Girls night / family night)

Can you enjoy a night in alone?

Do you have hobbies you do together?

What separate interests do you have just for you?

What are your DEALBREAKERS?

After you finish this list you will do one more thing with it . . .

A new vision

Now that you've made your list, I want you to create a story from it called a Vision Statement. This is the story of your future, written by you in the words that make your heart happy. You can write it to God or the Universe, to Life or even as though you are speaking to your future partner.

It would go something like this:

Dear Universe (or Dear Life or Dear ManofMyDreams)

I'm so excited to be spending time with my tall, handsome guy with a little scruff on his face. He always looks so good when he comes home in his jeans and work shirt. I love his casual style and nerdy glasses. My sister says I've finally met my intellectual, cosplay match. The day he met my dad I was so nervous, but when he gave him a firm handshake – and a hug (!) – my heart did a cartwheel!

The best thing about being with him is the time we spend on the couch, with one leg thrown over the other's, reading and sharing things from time to time. He, too, isn't comfortable with a lot of PDA, but at home he's so affectionate. I finally met someone who loves to pet my hair and it's the best thing ever.

When we disagree, he lets me have my feelings. He understands that I might overreact sometimes, but as long as I'm not being mean he manages to hear me out. I've been surprised at how much better this makes me at resolving things too. He's taught me a lot about agreeing to disagree and that it doesn't mean we don't love each other.

I feel so emotionally safe with him that our sex life just keeps getting better. He's adventurous and doesn't think I'm a freak just because I like sex! I like how confident he can be in the bedroom . . . it makes me feel like I really get to be the girl.

I'm so happy to have found my partner in crime, so to speak. I look forward to a future full of family and travel and sexy adventure!

Your statement would be much longer of course. I haven't included all of the sections here. But, as you can see, it's a positive celebration of your future. It's as though someone said to you, "How is it going? Tell me everything!!!" and you do! One of the PDFs in your file will be a "Helpful Statements" list that will help you come up with ways to phrase these things in a positive way.

The most effective way to do this is to type it first so you can mess with it and then, once you have finished this book and made any adjustments along the way, write it *by hand.* When desire and intention go from your brain, down your arm, through your hand and onto the paper, that is a very powerful, energetic event. You are "penning in" your future! Even if it feels like the corniest thing you have ever written, do it. One of my favorite lessons I learned from author and spiritual teacher Wayne Dyer is that the root of the word "enthusiasm" is *en theos,* or "with God." In other words, when you are excited about something and feel enthusiastic, you are feeling about it the way Source / God / The Universe feels about it. You are in alignment with your Highest Self. By the time you are done with this book and have your "first final" draft, you will have created a future story based on all of your highest wishes for yourself. It's a beautiful and powerful process.

In the meantime, while in "rough draft" mode, revisit your file often as you learn more about what a Triple-A Relationship looks like and what a life partnership can feel like. Some clients have recorded themselves reading it aloud and played it before bedtime or in the morning. This piece of informed, intentional writing plays an important role in attracting the love of your dreams. I am excited for you!

The Onion

• • • • • •

I like to call this lesson "The Onion" because it's getting to know the layers of someone. Just like an onion has layers to the center, a person has layers of their personality, and we get to know those layers over time. This diagram was used earlier in the "honor other" part of the introduction. This is where we go deeper into that conversation.

For our purposes, I'm breaking this down into four layers to get to know someone intimately. The reason it's so important to understand that you get to know somebody in layers is because firstly, in the extreme, creepy people can be really charming. So you want to get to know somebody before you get invested in them and really allow them into your world. Safety first!

The less extreme reason is that people are really good at covering up their issues and functioning over them. We all do it, and they don't come up until something triggers them. Everything can be going swimmingly, then you can step on somebody's wounds and then you've got a problem on your hands that's really, really difficult to deal with. Now, it might just be something that needs to be discussed, figured out and understood – and I'm going to give you some tools for that – but it's important to remember and to keep your mind open to the idea that you're just getting to know the layers of a person. This is who they were before they even met you. They're not the same as that outside layer. You're getting to know those deeper layers.

The number one reason that it is really important you understand this concept is because physical intimacy creates the illusion of emotion intimacy. It's really easy to know somebody on the outside layer, to get physically involved with them and maybe share things on the inside layer. You can think, "Oh god, I really know this person," but the truth is that all you know is the cover of the book. You know how they are in bed and you might know some intimate details about their life, but what you don't know is what those intimate details mean when it comes to their ability to relate to somebody else. Layer two, layer three and layer four are all about who they are as a person and what that means to you *in a relationship*. You're going to understand this really well by the end of this chapter – I promise.

You are going to learn to name the layers and have some tools to get to know those layers. I'm going to give you some good questions to ask that will be fun for him to answer instead of feeling like he's being grilled. Grilled – like an onion. Get it? OK.

The more efficiently you get to know the layers of someone, the more efficiently you're going to see how well he matches up to the list you made in the last chapter. So let's get on it.

Before we get into the details of this lesson, I want to make a disclaimer. As we're going further into this discussion, I'm making generalizations about men and women, what we want and how we behave. I want to say that, for ease of conversation, I will be saying "us," "we" and "women," and "them," "they" and "men." I want to acknowledge that I understand not everybody is the same, I'm going on years of experience of talking to men and women about their relationships and I'm drawing and teaching from the most common ground I can teach from.

The first layer

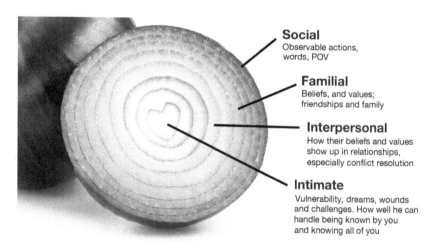

Social
Observable actions,
words, POV

Familial
Beliefs, and values;
friendships and family

Interpersonal
How their beliefs and values
show up in relationships,
especially conflict resolution

Intimate
Vulnerability, dreams, wounds
and challenges. How well he can
handle being known by you
and knowing all of you

OK, here again is your basic onion. Actually, this is kind of a cute onion because it has a little naturally occurring heart in the center, which I thought was adorable. (You can print one out at <u>sophievenable.com</u>.) The outside layer, the first layer, is called the social layer. This is the fun external layer where you meet somebody and get to know them by observing their actions and listening to their words. Your only job here is to be the observer. Observe how he communicates with you and with others. Observe how he talks about people who aren't there. You might even learn a little bit about his friendships if you happen to meet him in a situation where you're around his friends, but this is where you're getting an idea of how he communicates. You might get to know a little bit about his dating point of view, his family, his hobbies and stuff like that.

Becoming the observer is a mindfulness exercise in which you observe things around you and your own reaction to those things in a nonjudgmental way. At this level of getting to know someone, I'm not asking you to observe him and his actions to make assumptions, but to take things at face value and simply notice how you feel about them. There's no reason at this level to fill in the blanks for someone or make excuses for their behavior. You are simply acknowledging what is. So if he speaks to someone in a way that makes you uncomfortable, then notice that without making it OK because he's really good looking or because he loves the same music and dogs that you do.

To help you with becoming the observer and with all the concepts that are going to be brought forth in this chapter, I would like to introduce you to your two new best friends: interest and curiosity. As often as possible, whether it's around conflict, getting to know someone or learning about your own reaction to things, always come from a place of interest and curiosity. You can even use the sentences, "That's interesting. I'm curious about that." This will come up many times throughout this lesson because it's such an important skill, not just in your dating life, but in life in general.

There are definitely ways to get more information from basic questions. Say you ask somebody, "What do you do for fun?" That's always a nice question. And he says, "Oh I bowl." And you say, "Oh gosh, I'm terrible at bowling. One time I got the lowest score of everybody." Now you're talking about yourself. One way to change this so you can learn a little bit more about him is to say, "Oh, that's cool. When did you learn to bowl? How old were you?" or, "Is that something you do with your dad or your friends? Are you in a league?" Those are questions you can ask that will help you to learn more about this person. But remember: you're still just getting to know their story and what they choose to tell people they've just met. You're still just getting to know the cover of the book.

We tend to make a lot of assumptions at this level. We might think, "Oh, they're so nice and outgoing and friendly and fun," but we still need time to see if there's actual consistency there. This is also where we might say, "Well, he's a fifth grade teacher. He's got to be a good guy." Probably, but maybe he's not really a teacher or maybe he's a substitute and he taught fifth grade once. That's cool, but why is he exaggerating? What's going on there? At this level, we have to be very careful to not make too many assumptions.

If you start sleeping with somebody right away – and I'm not telling you whether you should or not – what you have to be aware of is that you know the cover of the book and you know who they are in the bedroom. The only things you have bridging the gap between those two things are emotional chemicals. There might be some deeper sharing going on there, but what you don't know, even though he might be sharing his hopes and dreams with you, is how do those things manifest in how he operates in the world in layer two and layer three? Pillow talk can seem very transparent, but doesn't give you the whole picture. You have to be careful not to fill in too many blanks just because you're sexually involved and you're getting emotionally invested. You could be hearing what you want to hear. That can be a trap. Remember: your job at this first layer is just to be the observer.

Now I'm going to explain a little bit about those emotional chemicals so that you can understand why this is so important. Here's a little science and biology lesson. A key hormone released during sex is called oxytocin. It's also known as the cuddle hormone, and it is key to human bonding. It increases our levels of empathy. What this means is that it lowers our defenses and makes us trust people more. Women actually produce more of this hormone than men. We don't really know why, but it means that women are more likely to let their guard down and fall in love with a man after having sex with him.

The problem is that your body can't distinguish whether this person is going to be the love of your life or whether they're just a one-night stand; oxytocin is released either way. So, while it will help you bond with the love of your life, it's also the reason you stick around in lesser relationships and stay in them longer due to momentum and sexual bonding. Men release happy chemicals when they orgasm as well, but the main hormone that is released is dopamine, which is a pleasure hormone. Because these happy hormones are contributing to your trust and bonding mechanisms, you have a perceived emotional intimacy on one hand, and on the other hand you have actual knowledge and intimacy. These are not congruent. What you need is to practice interest and curiosity over time.

The second layer

The next level at which we get to know people is the familial level. This is where you get to know more about their friendships and family relationships as well as their core beliefs and values.

Here you start seeing his close friendships and find out how many old friends he has. You can see if he and his best friend are really close. For example, would they actually drop everything to help each other out? How does he talk about his family? Is he close to his siblings? This is where you start noticing things like his level of empathy, his work ethic, his attitudes about gender, family and the world at large. You don't have to know somebody very long to be able to ask a few more questions that help you get to know them on a deeper level.

I'm going to introduce you to a concept that's part of a larger approach to marital harmony and good communication. This tool is called a "thinking question" and it's the best way to get an answer from a man after you've asked a feeling question. It's very simple. A good way to explain it is to use an example of how it might be employed in a couple's therapy session.

John and Mary are a couple who happen to be in the market for a car. Mary's decided that she wants a Toyota, whereas John is saying, "Maybe we should look at the Hondas first, or hey, the Subarus are looking really good this year." Mary, however, isn't having any of it. Her family always owned Toyotas and, well, she wants what she wants. So they go to a party where Mary starts talking to a guy. John and Mary are generally social with other people at parties; they don't have to be joined at the hip. However, John notices that Mary's over there having a very fun conversation with a nice-looking man. She bounces over to John and says, "Oh my gosh, that guy over there, Greg, he's in the auto industry. He actually writes about cars, and we're getting a Subaru."

Lo and behold, the rest of the night did not go very well. So there they are in their therapy session. If the therapist were to ask, "So John, how did that make you feel?" he's going to have a lot of emotions to untangle. The first thing he's going to be doing is protecting his ego because he's not going to want to say, "Well, I felt jealous," or, "I felt threatened by that guy." He's probably going to say, "Well, I don't know. It was fine, but that guy was kind of a jerk. He was a know-it-all or whatever," and that's where it's going to end.

Now, if the therapist says, "So John, in a perfect world, how would this conversation about the car have gone? How would the decision-making have gone?" That's going to get him back to the kitchen table where they're having the conversation. He can now think in terms of that scenario and say, "Well, I guess I would have liked it if we could have gone online and looked at some of the Hondas and Subarus and I could have felt as though my opinion mattered. That guy's fine. It's great that he knows a lot about cars and she wants to get a Subaru, but it would have been nice if she'd acknowledged that I recommended the Subaru too."

So now you've got a guy who is talking about his feelings. He's talking about his experience, how it affected him, how he would have liked it to have gone and nobody actually asked him how he was feeling. They just asked him to think about how he would have liked things to have gone. This is the difference between a feeling question and a thinking question. See how effective it can be in your communication?

Questions that you can ask early on that will help you get to know a little bit about this layer are things about their familial relationships and their belief systems. It won't feel like you're asking these things, though. It can be a little bit terrifying to say, "So, how's your relationship with your mother?" That makes him think, "What? Pressure!" You might want to ask instead, "So, what's the quirkiest thing about your mom?" or, "What's your favorite dish that she makes?" or, "What are holidays like at your house? Do you guys go out of town or do you still all go to your mom's house?" or, "What's the greatest adventure you ever went on with your dad?" or, "What's the best trip you've ever gone on with your family?"

Questions like this are fun to answer and they get somebody in their storytelling brain, so they tend to open up more. You're still learning about their family relationships, their belief systems and their values, but you're learning it in story form and getting to know him a little bit better. All the while, he's probably loving that you're asking him questions about himself and that you really want to get to know him. I guarantee you, if you use these types of questions, you will have an amazing amount of insight into this person's beliefs and values even after just one date.

The third layer

The third layer is their interpersonal layer. I also want to call this their interpersonal diplomacy layer because where you get to see this most obviously is in his conflict resolution skills. These involve the ways in which he handles not getting his way, having his feelings hurt or not liking something that you or somebody else have done or said. This is a very, very easy place to spackle in the cracks because what happens is this: in the beginning, you have a conflict and you may not like how he handled it, but you go ahead and spackle that in and just assume that you will instead avoid all conflict (which is, of course, impossible.) In the extreme, this can be an unhealthy emotionally abusive situation where you try to be perfect all the time so as to avoid any bombs going off, but that soon proves completely impossible as well. It's a really slippery slope to spackle things in and ignore possible red flags at this level.

Now, the good news is that a healthy male who may or may not have good conflict resolution skills is often really open to learning conflict resolution because they don't like conflict. They don't enjoy it, and if they have a way of communicating that can actually fix a situation, that's a dream come true for most guys. So you need some questions that you can use, at a point when conflict happens, in these first three months and beyond as this relationship is forming. Even though you guys are newly dating, getting to know each other and it's all fresh and shiny, you might have an argument over where to go to dinner. Maybe his blood sugar goes down and he can't make a decision; or it could look like you're flirting with somebody else even if you're not; or one of you could lock the keys in the car and the other one gets ticked off. I don't know. Things happen.

These are great learning opportunities to see who somebody is under pressure or in conflict or when they're drunk. There are tools you can and should be brave enough to use in that early part of the relationship as you're getting to know each other. It's always best to be sober and calm whenever possible, but we all know life doesn't always give us those perfect opportunities. Just make sure that your intent is to diffuse the situation and not to make it worse.

One great question I'm going to offer again is, "In a perfect world, how would that have gone?" Or, "In a perfect world, how would I have responded to you?" This, again, is going to get him thinking about a scenario. He's not dropping into his anger or his defensiveness immediately because you are asking him about making his world perfect or at least better. And he might have an answer that could really surprise you, or he might *not* have an answer. He might say, "Well, I guess you responded the best way any person could have expected to. I guess I was just mad and disappointed." And now you're having a conversation about feelings. Because you've learned a little bit about being the observer, you don't have to be super reactive and you can honor his feelings and say, "I'm sorry. I just want us to be happy, not mad and disappointed. How can we start over?" or, "Oh yeah, I guess I could have responded that way. Sorry I got so defensive."

What you were learning about in the second layer – those values he was brought up with – you're now learning how those affect him interpersonally and how they affect him in relationship. You're growing because you're not taking everything so personally and you're simply seeing him as a person who grew up in a different household from you. This doesn't mean you have to put up with meanness. In fact, if you remain the observer and ask these kinds of questions, you are way less likely to put up with emotionally abusive kinds of conflict.

The other thing you learn at this level is his level of empathy and a newer word in our language – compersion – which means the feeling of joy one has when they experience another's joy. In other words: the opposite of jealousy. This is his ability to be happy for you when you have a great day or a big victory. Strong, smart, dynamic women often struggle with relationships where their men cannot handle their success or their bigness. You can tell pretty quickly with a guy if he's insecure in that way by sharing some successes or fun stories and asking him things like, "Well, what would you wish for me?" or, "Can I show you what I've accomplished?" If your successes turn into big fights – or even little ones – every time, especially when you know you're not sharing in any kind of condescending way, this dynamic is not likely to change, unfortunately.

Conflict resolution is a learned skill. Many people grew up in households where nothing was ever resolved and no one ever felt heard or validated. That's why they have to work so hard in schools to make guidelines for it. But that's the beauty of choosing your primary love relationship. You're literally choosing your new future family and creating a new household. That's why this is such an important layer. It is the easiest one to sweep under the rug and spackle in because it's very scary. You'll find, however, that you're braver when you're asking these things because you're coming from a place of interest and curiosity and asking thinking questions to create an access point. It doesn't mean that you never talk about feelings, it just serves as another inroad to feelings.

If it's relevant, you could ask a hypothetical question like, "So, if your sister had said that, how would you have responded?" But what you're actually doing is asking from an objective point of view, as if to say, "I want to understand how this has been for you in the past and how you would like it to be now." This way, you really get to see if he has a true interest in getting along or if he's all drama all the time. Some people really thrive on conflict, and you can't control that. All you can do is create an opportunity for peaceful communication, which, in the best case scenario, leads to deeper intimacy in the relationship simply because you figure out ways to communicate instead of fight.

The fourth layer

Now let's look at the fourth layer. This is the deeply intimate layer where you are getting to know somebody's vulnerabilities. This is about his wounds, his challenges and his deepest hopes and dreams. These are things that take *time* to discover and understand. These are the parts of his personality and life experience that existed before you and will probably exist forever because the difference here is that wounds are not necessarily conflicts to be resolved. These are his pain and his story; this is part of his path. One of the ways we grow as human beings is to learn to respond instead of being simply reactive to our wounds when we get triggered.

This is the layer in which you're getting to know somebody who challenges you to be genuinely loving because you're now getting to know some deeper, more vulnerable, parts of them.

You may have noticed with other men that they can be terrified to show fear or vulnerability. A lot of times when they're afraid, they're angry, and when they're angry, they're angry. Even when they're sad, it can sometimes look like anger because that is a socially acceptable masculine emotion. This is just like the way that a lot of women are raised to never show anger, so we cry when we're mad, cry when we're sad, cry when we're scared, and I think we get the better end of the deal. Physiologically speaking, crying is actually a very healthy release and men could probably do with shedding a few more tears than they are used to. There are a couple of ways that this layer can be challenging. On one hand, which can be a good thing, he can be sharing his hopes and dreams with you. On the other hand, that dream could be that he wants to open an ice hockey rink in North Dakota, and you guys are currently living in

Florida. Meanwhile, you're exploding inside with this information and how it relates to you, but you don't want to shut him down and turn this around and make it about you. What you want to do is to continue to explore this.

You can ask questions like, "So, how long has this been your dream?" and, "Are there any other versions of this dream?" and, "How can I support you in this dream?" Now you're making it, again, a story and a situation. You're getting him into the thinking place, and you're also exploring how concrete and real this dream is. When you know this, you can decide whether it's relevant to you and whether you guys have to talk about how it fits in with your dreams. You do, however, want to be having that discussion based on things that actually come out of his mouth rather than a bunch of assumptions you make from hearing it in the first place. You can be supportive and get to know him better by actually asking him questions that support his dream. This way, you can untangle what's real about it for both of you and whether or not something has to be addressed.

Another challenge is when you're with a guy and suddenly he's reactive. Maybe he's been triggered by something and you don't really know what's going on. Now, if he's super self-aware, he could actually verbalize, "Look, you just stepped on some old stuff right now. My dad used to say that to me," and that's cool. More than likely, however, he's going to be overreacting to something you know was very small. This can make you very confused and it's hard to know what's going on. We've all done that, right? We've all overreacted to something and then realized that it's about something else. In this case, I'm not talking about somebody who's abusive or mean, but you want to be able to respond in a way that gets you more information about who he is as a person in this type of situation. This is really important information.

Because we're all human and nobody is perfect, the most common reaction to reactivity is to get very defensive and proclaim your innocence or look at them incredulously and tell them that they're being crazy. This is definitely not going to diffuse the situation. Here are a couple of little tips. Rule number one is that if somebody is being reactive and they say they need to go for a walk, let them go for a walk. There is actually a physiological reason for this. Rule number two is to remain as interested and curious as possible. Again, you're going to bring in some of those skills of being the observer and you're going to approach this with interest and curiosity. Firstly, though, I want to explain why you should let somebody go for a walk if they say they need to.

Oftentimes when we are triggered, particularly from childhood pain, what's being triggered is shame, and possibly rage about that shame. The problem with shame is that it's a spiral, as opposed to, for example, sadness. You can be sad, walk through sadness, and you will eventually get to the other side of it. You can face your fears and get to the other side of them. You can work through anger. You can run through it or punch pillows through it, but you can get to the other side of it. The problem with shame is that it's a spiral, and one of the only ways in the moment to step out of a shame spiral is to physically move your body.

So now we know that if somebody's asking to go for a walk, it's only going to help the situation. You might want to put a time limit on it, but you can step back as the observer and go, "OK, they are taking care of themselves and they're going to come back to me in a better place if they just go for a walk." The other thing that could be happening is if they're angry, they're getting the energy out of their extremities so that they can deal with some of that anger. Let them walk it off. That took me a long time to learn and I firmly believe that, male or female, if somebody needs to physically move their body, you should let them. Maybe while they're gone you could do a few jumping jacks or push-ups. It can only help.

Hopefully understanding this bit about shame will help you in your interest and curiosity around the situation. You want to be aware of your own feelings because neither one of you are going to benefit from being paralyzed and stewing in it. If you give each other a little room to move around, you can have some peaceful space to come back to and talk about what happened.

Some basic actions here that can help you in these situations are: one – check in and see if they need to go for a walk. Two – you can always ask, "Please tell me what happened for you." You want to hear in their own words what went on for them because you don't want to make any assumptions. You might have a completely different point of view of what was going on.

The fact that you're not in defensive mode and that you're coming from a place of interest and curiosity should take almost any situation down a huge notch. Now you're getting to know each other and you're constructively getting to explore how you can resolve things.

Other questions might be, "How can I know when this is going on for you?" "What does that look like?" "What can I do for you?" "What do you need from me when you're going through something like this?" He might actually say, "I need some space," and I think that's a reasonable request if somebody is asking for it and letting you know that's what they need in the moment.

Ultimately, all you can do is come from a supportive place. If coming from this place does not result in a lower temperature and, instead, brings about more aggression, then you might have a genuine problem on your hands. We're all going to make mistakes in relationships and we need to have peaceful ways to connect again without having to go through painful, damaging, emotionally draining fights. It's not OK for you to take the heat for his wounds, but, as somebody who cares about him, you can be kind and understanding and try to recognize it because that's what we do for people we love. We don't hit below the belt. We don't take their vulnerabilities and use them as weapons because those are hard, if not impossible, bells to unring. You are bound to run into some of these things as you get to know somebody, especially after three or four months when you are sexually involved, everybody's got the love eyes on and the illusion is that you should be able to read their mind and never hurt their feelings. And it's easy to get reactive in situations like this, especially if you're drinking. That's when you have to step back, be the observer and try not to say anything you can't unsay. If booze becomes a problem in situations like this, if there's always irreparable damage done, then booze is a problem, period. It needs to be addressed. Maybe this person is toxic for you emotionally or you can't drink together. That's a tough conclusion to come to, but better early on than at the wedding reception.

If you're doing this from the very beginning of a relationship – asking thinking questions, remaining the observer and trying to get to know the layers of a person from an outside perspective – you can better understand that who he is is not about you. It's not about you being more perfect or you completely avoiding conflict. This is *who he is* and you're simply uncovering these layers. You might be becoming the safe person for him that he can share his vulnerabilities with. This level of vulnerability is part of the beauty of being in an intimate relationship because – remember – this gets reversed too. You want him to be these things for you, to be a safe person for you to share your vulnerabilities with. But what you end up doing is teaching by example. When you start to create these tools for communication, he is very likely – if he's a good guy who's really interested in connecting with you, getting to know you and supporting you, your hopes and dreams – going to get the hang of this. He will quickly understand that there's a way you guys can actually communicate about things. That's what becomes this beautiful, safe, loving environment when you are physically involved too that is the most magical thing in the world. Being there for each other in your vulnerability is what emotional intimacy is all about.

Onion review

First we learned the four layers of getting to know somebody intimately – described with a diagram called The Onion. You learned about becoming the observer and what that means. You learned a little bit about oxytocin and its effects. We talked about thinking questions – there is a "Thinking Questions" PDF available to print out too. We talked about conflict resolution and went over a little lesson in shame and how it's a spiral. Overall, we looked at how coming from a place of interest and curiosity about hopes, dreams and old triggers can help to diffuse a reactive situation and ultimately bring you closer to a loving, emotionally intimate connection. So the good news is that your homework after this section of the book is just to ponder The Onion. All I want you to do is reflect. Print out the PDFs because they give you some handy notes and I also made very clear the questions you can ask to get to know each layer. So that's a useful tool. But I want you to see if you can apply this to your life in any way. For example, if something goes wrong at work, can you can approach your boss in a totally non-defensive way and say, "In a perfect world, how would this have gone?" Watch how they will get into the solution – they will be happy to tell you their vision. It's kind of fascinating how it all works. I also want you to think not just about relationships with men, but other relationships where you may have made a lot of assumptions along the way. Many women have a tendency to jump into female friendships quite quickly. We fall in love with that outside layer and then start sharing on a deeply intimate layer. However, we don't really know a lot about layer two and three and how these things affect this person's ability to be a good friend. Oftentimes, female friendships can get very, very intense and then completely blow up.

I just want you to reflect, think about what we've talked about and see how you can apply it to your past, then put some of it into practice.

The Dance

· · · · · ·

I like to call this lesson "The Dance." I call it this as opposed to "The Game" because in a game there's a winner and a loser. In a dance, however, you are both taking a little journey around the dance floor and there is a leader and a follower. In the same way that there are different steps to a dance, there are sometimes movements of a larger dance, for example, the ballet *Swan Lake*: I believe it has five movements. (I'm a dancer so I really like this metaphor.) There are three movements (or phases) to what I like to call the "Man / Woman Dance," and those movements are:

- Courtship
- Calibration
- Commitment

An important distinction in this lesson is that I'm going to be talking about men and women and male and female. I'm going to be making some generalizations and I want to acknowledge the fact that we're not all the same, but I also want to clarify a concept of what I'm calling "male" and "female." What I'm really referring to is **masculine energy** and **feminine energy** and we all, male or female, have both energies within us. If masculine energy is assertive, giving and linear, for instance, and feminine energy is receptive and fluid, both genders embody varying degrees of those qualities.

What I don't subscribe to is the idea that, if we were all just really honest with ourselves, women would be primarily feminine, men would be super masculine and everybody would hold tight to only those feminine or masculine traits. I don't believe that at all. I think what gives us our strength is that we harness both of those energies. If we look at a yin and yang symbol where yin represents the feminine and yang the masculine, there's a little dot in each side. That dot represents the other energy. I think we are, in a sense, looking for our same sized dot. So, if you are a very feminine woman with just a little bit of masculine energy, you might find yourself nicely balanced and very attracted to a man who has a lot of masculine energy and just a little bit of feminine energy.

Some women who have a lot of masculine energy want to enjoy their femininity but they also need somebody balancing who can bring more feminine energy. This man can still be in his natural degree of masculinity and she in her femininity and that creates a really nice balance, a lot of magnetic attraction and a perfect set of energies and ingredients to bring to the dance.

It's a theory

The following is a visualization of the "same size dot" theory. Take it for what it's worth.

possibly not the best match?

balanced match creating polarized attraction

Learning the dance

I'm going to talk a little bit about primal drives, particularly in men, so that you can get an objective point of view of where they're coming from. This will help you understand their behavior and their needs a little bit more, as well as the primary motivation behind each movement of "The Dance." What I also want to do is to remind you that, throughout all of this, the common theme here is that you have *choice*. You don't have to dance with somebody just because they asked you to dance. You don't have to make the dance work just because they asked you to dance. Remember, when somebody extends their hand to you, to invite you on a little journey around the dance floor, somebody has to lead that dance. However, it doesn't work without both of you and you have a choice as to whether or not to participate. This is not about some sort of requirement of you as a woman. What this is really about is understanding a man's way of thinking and processing the beginning, unformed relationship so that you can continue to dance, enjoy it and see where it goes from there without feeling confused, frustrated or lost. With that said, let's start learning about the "Man / Women Dance." Yes, it's all a bit corny and I've made up silly dance step names – but you won't forget them!

If you haven't already, I recommend printing out two PDFs from sophievenable.com (The Dance and The Dance Pitfalls_Tips) because that will make all of this easier to follow

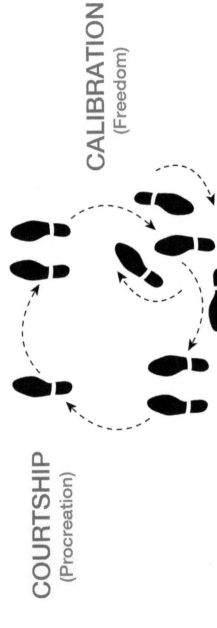

He's leading this Dance...

CALIBRATION
(Freedom)

COURTSHIP
(Procreation)

COMMITMENT
(Security and Consistency in Love)

Courtship

We're going to start with **Courtship**. Somebody's got to lead this dance, so the man is going to be the leader. But first, let's talk about primal drives in men. Some like to refer to the three Ps: procreate, provide and protect. Procreation is the drive for sex and perpetuation of the species. It's great that men have a very steady drive for procreation, because – as I like to say – if sex were complicated for both genders, we would be extinct. Providing and protecting are two pillars of masculinity that seem to date back very far, cross-culturally. These can be looked at as what it is that defines a man. The success a man likes to feel in courtship can be felt through succeeding at providing and protecting. This doesn't mean they have to provide shelter for you, pay all your bills, protect you from a lion or save you from a burning building. It can be something as simple as providing you some ease by picking up something for you or protecting you by walking on the street side. Sometimes this is looked at as simple chivalry. There's a reason for it, however, because it is an opportunity for him to be in his masculinity and provide and protect you in your femininity. You get to relax and be fluid and graceful in the world. It can also manifest in buying you dinner, providing you with food or providing you with sexual gratification. That's a huge success for a man.

When we look at **courtship**, I want you to remember the concept of providing and protecting and how this helps a man feel like a man, but not because you're weak and need protecting or you're incapable of functioning out in the world. You can go out in the world and kick ass. That's great. But any time you have an opportunity in a fun way to let a man provide for you and protect you, it's great to give him that opportunity. I love to let my man open my door for me. It's one of our little dances. He comes over to my side of the car. He opens the door for me. I look at him and say, "Thank you." Sometimes I give him a kiss. We have a little moment. When we're walking together, he might let me walk in front of him. If we have to walk single file for some reason, he never walks in front of me. Now, this might give him an opportunity to look at my butt, or it just might give him an opportunity to allow me to be more graceful in the world. This is all part of our fun little dance that we do in our relationship. It provides the opportunity to enjoy him being the man and me being the woman. It's romantic – and *romance* is what makes this relationship unique to your other relationships.

Let's say the initial drive in courtship for a man is procreation. A woman's drive in allowing herself to be courted is also about procreation, but also very consciously about seeking *security* and *consistency in love*. I don't want to say that men are not ever seeking *security* and *consistency in love* because they do get there, but that's not what they're thinking about initially. The thing to remember about men in the courtship stage is that men are very present and they're visceral. What I mean by that is that men need to feel things in present time. They're not visual in the way we are where we see the future. We literally see the movie of how this is going to play out. Sometimes, we're actually correct. But a lot of times, we're not. But we can be worried about or planning for the future when all he knows is that he likes being around us. He likes how he feels in our presence and that's truly all he knows.

Pitfalls in the courtship phase

One pitfall here is that you can be too critical. I honestly have to say if you're in the first few months of an unformed relationship and you're being critical, move on. Obviously you're not crazy about who this person is and he doesn't need to be with somebody who's critical right away. You guys just might not be a good fit. So, being critical can be as much of a problem for him at this stage as it is for you. But, for some reason, people stick around in situations like this and that's why I mention it. If you find yourself being critical, I really would say move on, for both of your sakes.

Another pitfall here is talking about the future. When you talk about the future a lot in this stage, you put pressure on the relationship and you bring the guy out of his present time where he's simply enjoying what's happening now. It starts to make them pull back. It's way too soon to be planning things. A lot of times, guys will be excited about you and, in the beginning, they'll say things like, "Oh, we should go to Bali next summer." Don't buy a bikini. Just know that when a man is talking about the future in this very early courtship stage, all that means is he really likes how he feels with you *right now.* And if he were to feel this way next summer, boy, wouldn't it be fun for you guys to go to Bali? It does not mean, however, that he has planned everything in between, meaning that he's not thinking about how long you guys will have been dating by then and where you're going to go bathing suit shopping and which airlines fly direct to Bali. I wouldn't go there. I would just take that with a little grain of salt and also take it as a sign that he really likes how he feels right now. That's awesome.

Along with talking about the future, it's easy to be too available in the beginning. What this means is that he still wants to win you. If you're completely available all the time, there's no challenge and I hate to tell you this, but that really takes a lot of the fun out of it for him. He wants to feel like there's a little bit of a success in asking you on a date and having you say yes. So, mirror his availability. In other words, let him lead the intensity and the depth of the relationship. Somebody has to lead this dance and I promise you that the way you're going to invoke a better response from a man is if you let him lead.

A side note: if a man is leading quickly into commitment, for example, if you've been dating for two weeks and he wants you to be his exclusive girlfriend and he's talking about living together, this is a huge red flag for being controlling. There is no logical reason a stranger should be that sure about wanting to be your partner that quickly. Generally, these guys know what you want to hear, it all seems very romantic and then you quickly realize the exclusivity only goes one way and he's telling you what you can wear and which friends you can hang out with. Please don't be seduced by this illusion of security and instant love.

Your dance step in the courtship phase

I call this the "charm and choose." Look at your priority list and *do your life*. You are assessing and *choosing* based on how he compliments your life and makes you feel. What I mean by "charm" is to be kind and encouraging. If you want to have a man feel great around you and be excited, respect him. Respect his capabilities, respect his ideas and respect his way of doing things. That doesn't mean you don't do things your own way. That doesn't mean you don't have your ideas. It just means you respect him and you're not immediately trying to have him always agree with you. You're not wanting him to do his life differently because the silly boy doesn't know how to live in a way that would work in a relationship. You just have to respect who he is and where he's at. If you don't respect him, that's OK, just don't hang out with him.

Then there's appreciation. Appreciation is manners and being kind. When he does things for you, when he provides or protects, definitely say thank you. Definitely flirt with him about it. Definitely give him some credit. Men really want to feel competent in front of you. There's nothing worse than a man being humiliated in his competence around a woman he's trying to court. It's such a bummer for a guy. Of course, they can handle it with grace. We've all been embarrassed before – but competence? That's a feeling he's really going to enjoy. He has fun when he goes out of his way, does something and she appreciates it. It's really fun and romantic. That's a sweet little dance.

Then there's warmth. Simply put: affection and sex, if you're at that point in your relationship. Respect, appreciation and warmth. RAW . . . easy to remember, men like it RAW. When a man has these things, and he's also enjoying giving these things, then he is going to start thinking more along the lines of security and consistency in love. But if the beginning of the relationship is work, pressure and a lot of future talk that he's not leading, then he'll bolt. Even nice guys get scared, and I'll explain that more in the next section when we start talking about calibration.

His dance step here is the chase, and that doesn't mean a never-ending chase where you're constantly running away from him. Your dance step here is the charm and choose. You're charming with your respect, appreciation, warmth and your kind encouragement. You are choosing by simply doing your life and choosing whether or not this is the way you'd like to be treated and whether you are really attracted to this guy and if he is mentally and physically stimulating to you.

Remember, you don't have to make it work with whoever chooses you. You want security and consistency in love with someone you want to give security and consistency in love to because you're crazy about him, not because he happened to choose you.

Calibration

This is a tricky phase, **calibration**. Calibration doesn't happen every single time in a noticeable way, but I would say this is a really common, consistent, predictable thing that happens in an unformed, early relationship. The definition of calibration is *to correct or adjust and compare to a standard, to determine the accuracy of something*. This doesn't mean he's comparing you to other women, it's more that he is comparing his life *with you* to his life *without you* in order to determine the accuracy of his assessment of your relationship. This is not conscious, he's not thinking, "I'm going to step back now and calibrate." This is an unconscious movement towards a normal level of courtship that can be maintained.

This is the time in the relationship where there's a noticeable difference in how often he's texting, calling and pursuing you. It's not that he isn't calling or texting or making plans, but he's doing it less often. It's as though he has slowed down the dance. You might now be doing a foxtrot instead of a cha-cha. He's still present and available, but you might start to panic at this point and read into what's happening.

Here's the thing. This kind of calibration – pulling back or asking for a little space – is not a bad thing. It's actually really natural. It represents his need to be present and visceral and to start considering giving up the main drive behind this movement of the dance: his freedom. I believe at a core spiritual level, we are all freedom seekers. We are all souls who want to be autonomous, to have freedom and to be able to grow and expand as people. But when it comes to our earthly dealings, relationships and especially potentially creating families, there is a stronger drive for security and consistency in love in women, and a stronger drive for hanging onto freedom in men. This does not mean that a man cannot feel freedom in a relationship.

As a matter of fact, that is exactly when he will usually commit: when he finds a woman with whom he can totally be himself and can feel a sense of freedom within that commitment. These are the men who are running to the altar because they are so thrilled to have security and consistency in love, as well as the ability to look to the future while maintaining who they are as a man. So, calibration is the most challenging time. This tends to make or break most connections.

There is, of course, the possibility that he's pulling away because he's less interested. But if you maintain your course and keep doing your life here, you're going to be able to assess that in a real way.

Pitfalls in the calibration phase

The biggest mistake that happens in this stage is that when a woman starts to feel him pulling away, she gets more clingy, worried and insecure. However, you have to own your assumptions and expectations. Maybe you guys always saw each other on Tuesday, but there is no always. There are no expectations. There is no, "But we always see each other on Tuesday."

You may have done this for a couple months, but perhaps seeing each other every Tuesday and Thursday and Friday and Saturday and Sunday is interfering with his life, his ability to get work done, his ability to work out, his ability to take care of himself and he's starting to feel that in his bones. He's starting to say, "Well I've got to manage my life a little bit," and we can learn from that. When the dance slows down, it's actually a good time for you to also assess how a relationship is fitting into your life and if you're still taking care of business.

This is also the time where a man is often dealing with fear, not just about giving up his freedom, but his realization of how deeply he is falling from someone. This can be really scary because, right now, he is actually considering giving up his freedom, and it's best not to ask someone to process their fear right in front of you. It's best to give him some space so that he can trust his own decision-making. Remember, he needs to assess. He needs to feel where he's at *in his bones* so that he can then consciously or unconsciously see if the two of you can move forward in this new recalibrated space where both of you have your lives going and you spend a normal amount of time together.

Your dance step in the calibration phase

Your dance step here is the "chill and choose." If you can just chill at this point in the relationship, you will be way ahead of the game. If you don't, if you get clingy, if you start complaining, if you start waiting for him all the time before you make plans, you have a much higher chance of actually imploding the relationship. The best thing to do at this time is to genuinely assume that everything is fine. It's not going to hurt you. It will hurt you to assume that there's something wrong, to play detective, to try to figure it out, to try to fix it, to try to be perfect and to try to see if he'll still text you to have lunch every Tuesday. That will mess things up. The best thing you can do is to assume everything is fine and do your life.

If he's doing the pullback shuffle, meaning he's texting and calling less but still making plans and still excited to see you, you have nothing to lose by chilling. I promise. Do your life, be kind and encouraging, make other plans, make plans with your girlfriends, take care of yourself, go to the gym, do everything that you need to do and let him adjust to you. When you see him adjusting to you, you're going to know without a doubt that this guy is into you and he wants to be in your airspace. By chilling out, I don't mean being rude, I don't mean being mad, I don't mean pushing him away. I still mean being kind and encouraging, practicing RAW, taking care of yourself, doing your life, but still letting him lead any conversations about the future.

This might seem really annoying, but if he starts to talk about the future or if there's something that you bring up around the future, just keep everything as hypothetical as possible. Use expressions like "wish," "wonder," "hope to," "I could imagine myself" or "I would be totally willing to go rock climbing in Yosemite." I know this seems like you're dancing around something or being a little bit too cautious, but it won't hurt you to be less than 100% sold on the future. You want him to claim your future. You want him to ask you to clear your books and have it be his idea. When you face things in a way that makes it clear that both you and he know that you have your life and you can make things happen with or without him, then you have options. That's what's going to stimulate the part of him that continues to want to provide, protect, procreate and succeed at these things so that he knows he's your man. Which brings us quite organically to commitment.

Aah, commitment

It's the thing women think men don't want to do. However, healthy males who are with a woman who they have fun with and have warmth, affection, sex and understanding with, who feel respected and who feel as though they're with somebody that they respect – it's these guys who are running towards commitment. They love it. They're happy. They want to be there. So, the drive behind commitment actually becomes the same for both of you here. This is where you are both thinking the same way. He's really interested in security and consistency in love, especially now that he's had some time to know what this love with you specifically feels like, and he's also had some time to experience what it's like without you. He knows that when you're not available, he misses you and he wants to be with you.

I want to remind you that the Latin root of the word "relate" means "to come back to." I like to say that you have to *unlate* to *relate*. Unlate's not really a word, but I'm going to say it anyway. It's this theory that says space, not always being available, having your own life and your own interests can help bring air into the relationship, which helps the fire burn. If you take all the air out, the fire is snuffed. This is the part of the relationship where you've established that the two of you being in this relationship is your happy place. You may have predicted it way back when you first met each other, but he didn't. He needed time to get here and we can learn from that. We can learn from being more present, more visceral, not spackling or filling in blanks and truly experiencing the relationship for what it is. Alongside this, doing a little calibration every day, saying, "Do I like how I feel with this person? Do I respect him? Do I feel affection for him? Do I appreciate him? Do I feel appreciated? Do I feel respected?"

All this calibration should be part of your process to getting to commitment as well. The greatest thing about finally having the DTR (define the relationship) talk or getting into commitment is that now it's safe for both of you to talk about the future. Now you can go buy a bikini for Bali. (Can you tell I'm really itching to go to Bali?) But it's more than planning vacations. Hopefully up to this point you've been doing your homework and getting to know the layers of this person, as well as revealing the layers of yourself so that now, as you look to the future together, you are aware of the things you want. That means asking yourself some questions: Do you want to get married? Are you OK with just living together? Are you looking to have children? How do you see your future in that way? Hopefully the two of you have revealed some of those things, so that the decision to say yes to commitment is informed and based on you having shown him who you really are, as well as observing who he is and how he lives his life.

Pitfalls of the commitment phase

The biggest pitfall here is forgetting that courtship and calibration continue for both of you. Courtship, the dance, the providing, the protecting, the being kind and encouraging, the not being available every second he asks, the doing your own life – this all continues. It's what keeps you interesting. It's what keeps him interesting. It's what gives you something to talk about. It's what keeps the fire burning.

Nobody wants to be somebody else's life raft. Think about any other relationship in your life. Maybe your mother, a sister or a brother, maybe a girlfriend who is needy to the point of making you feel like you can't possibly be enough for them and who needs you to be available to them in a way that makes you feel bad for living your own life. Nobody wants to feel that way. Even when a man is deeply in love, he tends to be more focused on one thing at a time. So if he's at work, or practicing his guitar, or exercising, he may not want to be on his phone having a conversation. Men tend not to be as conversational as we are. Now, maybe he was in the courtship stage, but, again, we're talking about livable levels of the dance and the courtship. Try to remember that making somebody feel as though they owe you something or as though you can't function without having heard from them can make them feel really uncomfortable. Frankly, it's just not sexy. He can't be your life raft and also be your lover. It's too much. You don't want to have to mother him and be his lover. Blech! That doesn't feel good either.

It's interesting. A man loves to be a hero. He wants to provide, protect, succeed and be your hero, but he doesn't want to be your life raft. These are two very different things. If I am being a life raft, I have to stay right here all the time just to make sure you can keep your head above water. Being a hero is him knowing you can breathe with or without him, but that you want him there because the way he loves you makes your life so much better. He should still be doing the chase and you should still be doing the charm, and he might be doing a pull back here and there and you might be doing a pull back here and there because you need a little space. But, at the same time, both of you are choosing each other every day. And that is truly how relationships go on forever.

Relationships don't reach forever status because somebody made a promise that they would be in love with you 30 years from now. Nobody can promise that. However, the two of you can be loving for 30 years and wake up one morning and go, "Holy crap. We've been doing this for 30 years! That's so amazing." This is what inspiring and beautiful relationships are: the continuing dance of the masculine and the feminine, the attraction, the giving each other room to be yourselves and to calibrate when you need, to figure out what you want, and to talk about the future together because you've established that you love being around each other.

Ultimately, the commitment you both want, and the type of relationship you both want, is the same. You just have a different route and a different set of dance steps to get there. I wouldn't tell you to let him lead if I didn't think it was good for you. Quite honestly, I don't think there's a choice. Men take a little longer to get there than we do and when they do take their time to get there, it's actually a very healthy thing. You simply cannot ask or convince another human being to move forward emotionally. It's impossible. All you can do is create room and safety for them to do so. This period of calibration is a really healthy thing for you as well. This is where, if you can not worry about trying to figure him out and turn the focus to you, then you can decide whether or not this is a good match for you.

So, now you're in this committed relationship. That doesn't mean the consideration is over. You can get to a point of commitment in a relationship because everybody wants to feel nice and safe there. Then you really get to ask, "How does this look? How does it feel when we're looking towards the future together?" In the next chapter, we're going to talk about how you know whether or not it's the real deal. What is it that makes a relationship truly flourish and continue in the long term?

A quick review

Let's do a quick review of the dance. He is leading. We start with courtship, and the primary drive behind courtship is procreation. Success in courtship, for him, has to do with feeling successful in providing and protecting, as well as feeling respect, appreciation and warmth. Success for you here is that you are enjoying being courted and that you're happy with how you're being treated. This generally leads to a calibration which is primarily driven by his need to hang on to his freedom. Success in this stage is, for him, a feeling of freedom within the relationship while still feeling successful even though the courtship and dating has been brought to a level that is manageable. Success here for you is to continue to do your life, take advantage of this calibration time for yourself, make sure that you're happy and always let your actions show that you have options and that you, too, have a life.

If you get through the calibration stage, you are generally moving into at least the first stage of commitment where both of you are driven by a desire for security and consistency in love. Success here is about both of you continuing to do this dance of courtship, calibration and commitment. Success here is about choosing each other every day because you are each other's happy place.

The Real Deal

• • • • • •

A wise and beautiful man named Paul Newman was once asked, "What is the secret to your long-lasting marriage?" He replied, "Proper amounts of lust and respect."

The Real Deal is the last piece of the puzzle in this book. You are now clear about the qualities you're looking for in a partner, and now you'll be getting clear on what qualities in a relationship can lead you to a real deal love that lasts. We've talked about your part, which is having an accepting and positive view of yourself and your life as an individual. That's huge. And we've talked about getting any negativity out of the way of the dating process or even simply the decision that you want to be coupled. You are probably getting really good at reframing. We've also gotten really clear about your initial list of qualities you would love to find in a partner. This list is about to get a little longer, or possibly adjusted and rephrased a bit. We've also talked about getting to know the layers of someone, as well as the dance you are doing while getting to know these layers and moving into that early committed stage as the relationship goes from being unformed to a bit more defined. I want you to understand what it means and how to tell if you're headed towards a real deal kind of relationship – even if you haven't met anybody yet. This is because this concept is so important in forming the foundation of a flourishing, lasting relationship that it must become part of your intention. You don't get a relationship, you grow a relationship. It's like a garden. You can choose the plants and give them a place to hang out, but then you have to tend to that garden just the right amount. Those first few weeks are a little tentative and dicey. You don't want to just yank the whole thing out of the ground because a few things go wrong or desperately overwater it because a few things go right! You can't undo poison in the soil either if you go too far with the weedkiller. (I may be going too far with my metaphor here, but you get the idea.)

In *The Onion* chapter, we looked at how it's easy to do damage when we get reactive with someone as we get to know their layers. We also discussed how it's easy to get invested before we really know someone. So if you can really get to know the feeling and image of what the real deal is for you, you are going to care for it and tend to it and give it the best chance possible to last and be beautiful. When you meet someone, or if you are in the early stages with someone now and are exploring this relationship further, I want to give you three overarching concepts to be conscious of when considering this as a long-term relationship.

There are lots of relationships that can be fun for six months, a year, or even 18 months, but at that point you're usually looking towards a deeper commitment. This could be in the form of living together, marriage, or just planning lots of future trips. Either way, your lives are becoming intertwined. These three elements are truly the ingredients that sustain a relationship over time. And, just because I like visuals, I would like you to note that the most stable architectural shape is an equilateral triangle. A real deal relationship has to have stability in order for it to grow and flourish over time because stability creates safety. The kind of safety we're talking about is emotional safety, because the most damaging things that can creep into a relationship are insecurity and resentment.

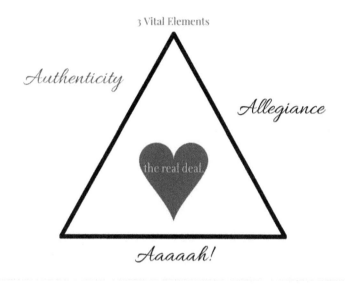

So just as there are three stabilizing sides to a triangle, there are three stabilizing qualities that create emotional safety and the foundation for a healthy, loving, sexy relationship. These AAA elements (to make it easy to remember) are **authenticity**, which is the ability to be yourself; **allegiance**, which means you feel that this person has your back and is on your side; and **aaah**, which is the passion. Without all three of these elements, there isn't the stability and fertile ground that allows growth in the relationship. I'm very confident that any issue you come up with can fit into one of these categories. When a relationship develops with these qualities early on, it has all the conditions that promote adoration, bonding and, ultimately, continued commitment. We're going to go over these qualities, learn what they look like in action and see how you can create opportunities for them. Using the Triple-A Relationship worksheet, we will be finding examples of these feelings in your life so you can recognize them in your body and know what it feels like when you have them, as opposed to when you don't.

If you haven't yet, print out both PDFs so that you have the Real Deal triangle to look at and make notes on if you want to, alongside your Triple-A Relationship worksheet.

Authenticity

So, what does it mean to have authenticity in your relationship? This boils down to whether or not you are able to be yourself. I have a seemingly silly example I often use about my second date with my boyfriend. He asked me if I would like a beer. It seems so stupid to me that I had any resistance to admitting this – because I felt sort of uncool – but I stayed true to myself and I said, "Well, I really only like one beer." And he said, "Oh, which one?" And I said, "Heineken." And he goes, "My woman," and proceeded to order two Heinekens. It turned out to be this really fun moment that we had and I'll never forget it because it was a real hit for me. I realized it felt good and worked out well to just be authentic. If that isn't a little sign from the universe to just be yourself, I don't know what is. So I kept up the discipline of being honest about my likes, my dislikes, my thoughts and my opinions as we were getting to know each other. I had an old habit of wanting to be and think and like everything that somebody else might want me to be and think and like. This relationship was a big practice for me in making progress in that way. That's one simple but profound example of a way you can create opportunities for this, which is to be your full self. As we've talked about so much in this book, do your life. Keep your priorities in mind. Know that you are a beautiful, multifaceted product of your background and your upbringing and you want to reveal the layers of yourself in an authentic way. You also want to get to know him and his layers in an authentic way, as he is coming from his own background and his own upbringing. This brings me to an example of how you can create authenticity from his point of view. Again, this is very simple, yet profound.

Something I've noticed my whole life with men, whether it's father, brother, friend or boyfriend, is that when they are in an unstable or inauthentic relationship, they always change how they are or what they're saying when their girlfriend walks into the room. Now, if it's a group of guys who are talking about something crude or making a dirty joke or whatever, they might not want to continue to speak that way in front of you out of respect, but there's still a way to be authentic. Your guy can let you in on the joke without selling out one of his buddies if he knows it's safe to do so. If you were to ask my boyfriend, "What is different about this relationship than any other relationship in your life?" he'd say, "I never have to change what I am saying or how I am being when she walks into the room." He expresses that as one of the greatest gifts this relationship has brought to him. When he tells other men that, and he has, they nod with such a knowledge of what he's saying. Some nod in agreement, "I know, isn't that the best?" Some nod with a wishful, wistful look as if to say, "God, I wish I had that." Like I said in the last lesson, when a man feels like he has the freedom to be himself, it's an exhilarating feeling in a relationship. It feels like freedom within the commitment. This might be easier for me to understand because I grew up with brothers and tons of their friends, so I'm used to how guys behave. I also love men and I tend to enjoy a raunchy sense of humor, but – more importantly – I never want to make a man feel bad about being a man. Men are visceral creatures. They are sensual creatures. They love food, women, cigars, whiskey and beautiful cars. Whatever their sensual favorites are will probably not change. I'm not saying it's OK to be rude to you in any way, but to get angry at a man for noticing another woman's beauty is like him getting mad at you for saying, "Wow, those are beautiful shoes." He isn't thinking, "Hey, you've got good shoes at home. Why do you have to notice that?" There is beauty and art everywhere and women are beautiful. To quote Jenna Marbles, "Women are majestic fucking creatures" and you are one of them. He's been noticing women since he was born. It's not going to change because he met you. You want him to love women because men who love women want to treat them well. And you are his favorite because he can be himself with you, you have his back and you have chemistry. You see where I'm going with this?

You absolutely have a right to your boundaries and to let him know how you want to be treated, but, while it's one thing to get upset with someone for their behavior and ask them to change it, it's another thing to shame them for how they think or feel. The more you can give him positive feedback for being authentic and the more you can take the opportunity to reveal yourself authentically, the more you're going to create trust and emotional safety in the relationship. If you continually pretzel yourself and dim your light or adjust yourself to be what you think he wants you to be, you're not going to feel known, you're not going to be behaving from your most authentic self or connecting with him from an authentic place. That creates insecurity because you're always trying to second-guess the right way to be instead of knowing that the only way to be is *real.*

Recognizing authenticity

Take a look at your worksheet. Now, firstly, I want you to remember someone, a friend, family member, teacher or former lover, who you felt like you couldn't be yourself around. Maybe you had to hide a part of yourself or not say certain things. I want you to be very aware of what that feels like in your body, in your shoulders, your face and especially in your chest. Do you feel hot, cold, tight, open, heavy, light, buzzy, small? I want you to write down three or four words that describe that feeling. Now I want you to think of an example of someone you can really be yourself with, like your best girlfriend or your sister or brother or maybe one of your parents. Write down that person's name and think about a time you were sharing with that person and being yourself. How does it feel in your body to be around them? Do you feel light in your chest? Do you feel happy? Do you feel energized? Does it feel like this person is an energy giving person as opposed to energy taking, and how does that make you feel about them? Do you feel motivated to embrace everything that they are? Are you accepting of this person because they are accepting of you? Those are the feelings in your body, heart and mind that I want you to recognize. I want you to put words to them now. Don't take this to mean that you're going to reveal everything to this man that you would reveal to your best girlfriend. There are things to process with your girlfriends that you don't necessarily process with your guy, and

I'm going to discuss that more in the Allegiance section. Becoming aware of what it really feels like for you to be truly authentic with somebody is going to make you aware of that feeling in your body. This means when you do start revealing yourself and your layers, and you get his response to that, you can check in with your body and see if it feels the same or even better. You say to yourself, "How does this feel? Am I starting to feel a little lighter every day around this person and a little less nervous? Do I feel a little more like I can reveal myself and that he accepts who I am? Or do I start feeling like he's disapproving of who I am and he's trying to convince me to think, be and like things a different way?" If so, that should be added to your list of dealbreakers.

Allegiance

Let's talk about **allegiance**. Allegiance is about loyalty and devotion to someone, but it's bigger than that. It actually means to be *committed* to a *common* cause – and that cause in a relationship is your growth and expansion. It's about feeling as though you have somebody on your side who cares about your growth as a soul. This also includes whether or not somebody is loyal to you in terms of monogamy (assuming that's your agreement,) but what I'm really looking at here is something less tangible. It's actually the foundation for that, because someone who's on your side doesn't want to betray your trust. The question is, do you feel like this guy has your back? That can be anything from sticking up for you if you have an altercation with someone, to bringing something to work that you forgot for an important meeting. Being committed to each other's expansion includes your partner supporting your hopes and dreams, believing in you and genuinely caring about your life satisfaction, maybe even helping you achieve it where possible. You see, someone can give you gifts, do things for you, say nice things, be affectionate and spend quality time with you, but, if he doesn't want you to get a college degree because that's threatening to his ego, that's not love. That's fear. We are expanding souls in an expanding universe and if either of you must stay small to be worthy of the other's love, that will not feel like allegiance and it will breed resentment and unhappiness.

Having somebody's allegiance and being loyal to each other is not always about agreeing with each other. That would be "alliance." It's about honoring each other's opinions, even if you don't agree, and still feeling like that person is on your team. They might not agree with you, but they can still support you because that's part of you, and they love you. This element is only created, so to speak, by being it and by asking for it. Here's a simple example. Let's say you really want to start a workout program and your boyfriend doesn't agree with how you're going about it. Let's say he thinks you should be lifting weights, but you want to do cardio because you know you'll show up. He may not agree with you, but you want and need him to still be rooting for you. So, your job here is not to convince him that you're right, but to be clear with him that you don't need him to agree with you, you just need him to be encouraging. "Let me try it my way and see how it goes." "I just need to feel like you're on my side." That's how a relationship becomes a beautiful support system in your life instead of yet another adversary or parental figure to whom you have to prove yourself. Think about that for a minute. If he's still on your team and he is still encouraging you even while disagreeing with what you're doing, then he is honoring your desire to try something your way and he's supportive of you and your endeavors. And if and when you do decide to ask him about lifting weights, it's not about losing an argument, it's just about getting his input because you know he wants to help.

That's how you ask someone to be on your side. You're not asking them to agree with you, you just want them on your team and to believe in your competence. Looking at his point of view, reverse the scenario in your mind and add to it that piece about how men really need to feel competent in front of you. Think about how you can be on his side in that way. Even if you see how something could be done or how it needs to go, give him an opportunity to solve it his way. That's the practical situational example. Now I want to give you the four most important intangible words regarding any relationship.

Trust each other's intent. This is the foundation for all conflict resolution in any relationship. It's what helps to avoid painful things being said in an argument and hurtful bells being rung that can't be unrung. If you've been seeing this person for two, three or four months, I'm hoping and assuming that you've been keeping your list in mind as well as your dealbreakers. This way, you are only moving forward with someone whose layers continue to show you that he is a kind and well-meaning man as opposed to spackling in a bunch of red flags and trying to turn a narcissist into a loving boyfriend.

I'm going from the starting point of a *kind* and *well-meaning* man, but it is inevitable in relationships, especially an intimate and vulnerable one, that the other person will trigger some wounds or insecurity in you or just plain piss you off. Even good people do disappointing things sometimes. I have an example story I use a lot. I call it "Stepping On Your Foot." We can all relate to someone stepping on our foot by accident and having the pain long outlast the quick apology that follows.

Think about when someone steps on your foot and they apologize. The apology does not make the pain go away. Your foot still hurts, sometimes for days. But it wouldn't be cool for you to keep going back to that person and explaining how clumsy they are or how thoughtless they were because all they can do is continue to apologize. You want to be careful about inadvertently accusing somebody of being a horrible person by implying they may have done it on purpose or that they are careless at their core. That would not be trusting intent. At a certain point, you have to take responsibility for being on this game board called life, and sometimes shit happens. You have to own your pain, accept it and hopefully get over it. This is exactly what I was referring to when I said you don't necessarily want to process everything with your guy that you process with your girlfriends.

Sometimes you have to call a friend and say, "Can you believe he stepped on my foot?" and then she can say, "Oh my god, that really sucks," but remind you that he probably didn't mean to step on your foot and hurt you. It's not going to do you any good to take all the "How could you?"s and the "Can you believe it?"s to him because that means he has to defend his character. That is not how to make your man feel like your man. You have to process it, get out your frustrations and then go to him with an opportunity to make it right, like, "I know it was an accident. Can you be more careful with X, Y, Z next time?" He can say, "Yes, of course," which gives him an opportunity to step up and be your hero again. This is how accepting an apology in a rational way can make you feel like you're on the same team.

This is probably the greatest opportunity for growth and emotional maturity that comes from intimate relationships. Trusting intent means we don't go down the road of character assassination. You either trust that this person is a good and well-meaning person or not. And if not, why are you there? This is where the difference between visceral and visual processing that I talked about in men and women comes into play and can be toxic. When a man disappoints us and we worry that he did so because he doesn't care about us or no longer finds us attractive, we can take that all the way down the road to thinking *he really doesn't want me and this is how he's always going to treat me.* After this, we could go to him and accuse him of doing whatever he did for that reason, and he will likely take that accusation very literally. His thought process will be, "But I've spent these months showing you how much I care about you and everything's been good. Now I've made this mistake that I'm apologizing for, but you're telling me that I don't care about you at all and I can't apologize for that because it's simply not true. This is crazy."

This is why, culturally, we go down the road of thinking that men are thoughtless jerks and women are crazy when it's not that way at all. Perfectly rational women can get scared when something triggers their insecurity. It happens. And perfectly nice men can be thoughtless when they're being single-minded, careless or if they're uninformed about your needs. All this can be reversed in the genders, of course. I've actually been in a relationship like that, and I can tell you it *kills* the love. Not trusting intent kills the love because it creates fear, and love and fear can't exist in the same space. Trusting someone is risky, but love is risky business. When you give someone the benefit of the doubt, at least you know that you tried and that you created opportunity for resolution. *That* is being on the same team.

Some useful tools

To help you be a good teammate, I want to give you two useful tools that you can take into your next relationship. The first one is called "I statements." You may have heard of I statements, you may have heard them joked about in sitcoms or referred to on talk shows, but I statements are actually a great tool and they require a little bit of discipline. An example is instead of saying, "You hurt my feelings," an I statement would be, "I felt sad when you did that." What it does is demonstrate ownership of the feeling. Things like, "I feel frustrated when you are late," or, "I feel sad when you use that tone of voice," are examples of I statements. This is where I statements and trusting intent will save your relationship, whereas the opposite will break it.

Let's say you've accepted an apology, but you're still spinning because you're afraid of what the motivation behind the egregious act was. You have to acknowledge your fear and take ownership of that fear. For example, let's say my boyfriend and I are at a party, we're drinking wine and I'm in the middle of telling a story that's more of an expression of my philosophy and some brilliant conclusion I've come to. I'm having a fun, wine-fueled time expounding upon my theories, and he comes up and interrupts me, changes the subject and directs everyone's attention to something hilarious that's happening on the other side of the room.

Cut to 10 minutes later, he can tell something's wrong. I say, "I'm hurt because you interrupted me in the middle of the story," and he says, "Oh gosh, I'm sorry. It was just such a commotion and I'm kind of buzzed and I didn't realize. I'm sorry. I love you." OK. I can accept that. But now, my fear is that he knew what story I was telling and thought I was embarrassing him because he doesn't really think I'm that smart and he did it on purpose. I'm afraid he thinks I'm embarrassing and not smart. The only evidence of this is his action, which he's already explained, and if I'm living by the premise that he's a kind and well-meaning man, then I have to trust his intent by giving him the benefit of the doubt. I need to own it. I need to say, "I know you're telling me the reason you did that was because you were buzzed and it was chaotic, but my fear is that you actually heard my story and wanted to interrupt me because I was embarrassing you. Sometimes I'm afraid that you don't think I'm smart."

With this, he can come towards me. He's not on the defensive. He wants to take care of my fear. He can assure me, let me know that I don't embarrass him and let me know he thinks I'm smart. Because I haven't accused him of being a horrible person, he might even promise that in the future he'll be a little more aware of interrupting me. I'm now going to take this a step further.

In that moment, even after he's assured me, it still hurts like my foot still hurts, and I'm still bummed that it happened at all. I can choose to go on and on about how inconsiderate it was and about how *if he really did respect me, he never would have done that*. But what's my goal? Is it possible to go on until he feels so bad that my foot actually feels better? Can I give him the pain? No. It doesn't work that way, and I don't want to do that. I want the relationship. He has confirmed to me that he really does think I'm smart and he does care about what I have to say, even if his actions were disappointing. It's now time to put on my big girl pants and accept the apology.

People are going to make mistakes, even when they love you. When you express yourself with I statements without accusing the other person of being a bad person or attacking their character, you can get the emotional need met of calming your fears and creating more safety and intimacy by trusting their intent. Let that be a cautionary tale: if I were to layer that much meaning onto every interruption, I wouldn't have a boyfriend because that is exhausting. So choose your battles, as they say. And, for the record, I'm the interrupter in the relationship. Shocking, I'm sure. So this was a totally hypothetical story.

The second tool I will give you will help you choose your battles. Sometimes we need to vent, so your tool is calling a friend first. When in a relationship with a man, I recommend not venting to him about him. Call a friend with all the "he statements." "He did this." "He did that." Vent to someone else. He does not need to hear you talk about how thoughtless and stupid it was that he was late or forgot your sexiversary. Let her hear you out and then hopefully, if she's a friend who likes your relationship and cares about your happiness, she will remind you how he didn't mean to be an ass or that you just need to let him know that it's important to you that he's on time because that feels loving and respectful. So, by the time you call him and say, "Something happened that I would like to talk to you about," you can submit a clear and tangible complaint and request new action in the future.

I know it seems like it would be more satisfying to stress to him how thoughtless he was, but I'm telling you, if you have decided that this is a good and well-meaning man, then you don't need to be beating down his character. You don't need to let somebody do that to you either. Just like the element of authenticity, concerning being able to be yourself, it's one thing to be upset about how someone behaved. It's another to shame them about how they think or accuse them of poor character. That is poison in a relationship.

When a man is in a relationship where he feels that no matter how he screws up, big or small, he's going to be run through the ringer, he's going to stop trying because he feels like he's not getting any credit for being a good person, so why bother? But when he's in a relationship where he knows if he screws up you will come to him with it, he will appreciate the peaceful opportunity to apologize. By doing this, you are showing that you trust him and give him credit for being a good person, therefore you're setting him up for success in the relationship. This isn't going to make him be lazy about it and become a worse person. It's going to inspire him to be his best person. He's going to feel like he can be real with you, even if sometimes he's not perfect. And that is freedom, and that is sexy.

Recognizing allegiance

All this talk has probably reminded you of someone in your life who you couldn't apologize to or someone who you really felt wasn't on your side. I want you to take note of what that feels like for two reasons. One, so you don't put up with it and two, so you remember how bad it feels to someone else. So, when someone in an argument is saying to you, "I don't know what else you want. I swear I want to fix it. I'm on your side," let that wake you up. Realize you have to trust his intent. And if you find yourself saying things to someone else like, "I'm sorry, I'm on your side," and he says, "But you wouldn't have done that if you really cared," you can just stop in that moment and recognize that's the problem right there. It's that you're not on the same team and you don't trust each other's intent. That is a fundamental issue in a relationship and needs to be fixed immediately, often with third-party help.

On a happier note, I want you to go ahead and think about somebody in your life who is always on your side. Even if it's just a moment in your life, like a teacher who you really felt had your back in a situation or was rooting for you. It could be somebody who's in your life all the time or it could just be an example of a single moment. Think about that person and what it felt like to have somebody on your side, especially if you can come up with an example where they didn't necessarily agree with you, but were still on your side. This doesn't mean you're on different teams. When you don't always agree with each other but still have each other's back, that's a mature relationship.

So close your eyes and think of a great moment with that person and breathe into it. Does that give you a grounded feeling? Does it give you strength? Does it make you feel emotionally safe? Does it give you a light feeling in your chest or a happy feeling? I want you to write down anything you can feel in your body that you can recognize and name. If you can name and recognize that feeling, especially in opposition to the other experience we explored, when you come to a crossroads with anybody in your life, you'll be able to tell the difference between what it feels like when somebody's on your side and when they're not. You won't be confused by a mysterious problem. You'll know what it is and be able to address it from there.

You can say, "Whoa, we need to be on each other's side," and then you can create opportunities for that and see what it looks like for each of you. In the worst-case scenario, you know you really tried.

Aaaah!

The third – and most fun – A in our Triple-A Relationship is the Aaaah. This is all about passion. If the previous two elements were about proper amounts of respect, this is all about the lust. This is important and precious because it's what makes this relationship unique. The passionate part of your relationship, your sex life and your attraction to each other are really, really, really important. Like a garden, you don't just get it. You have to nurture it and take care of it or it will peter out.

So, what makes passion burn over time? For this answer, I turn to science. The answer lies in the fire triangle, a basic scientific explanation of what ignites fire. The three elements that ignite and keep a fire burning are heat, fuel and oxygen. For our purposes, the heat is your physical attraction. It could be mental attraction. Either way, it's a sexy feeling, a spark. This is the first thing needed to ignite the fire.

The Passion Triangle™

The Passion Triangle

Breathing Room
physical & mental

Spark
attraction, novelty, adventure

OXYGEN HEAT

FUEL

Love = Authenticity + Allegiance
experienced with consistency

©2016SophieVenable

The fuel is the love. Appreciation, adoration, respect — all the loving acts that build the foundation of all of your affection for each other. I go so far as to define love as the experience of **authenticity** and **allegiance** over time. The oxygen is the air, or space, that you allow in the relationship. Remember that thing about unlating in order to relate? That's very important to keep a fire burning over time. Let's take each element one at a time.

The heat

This is mainly your physical attraction, but it also includes shared novelty, variety and fun. Physical attraction may seem like a surface quality in a relationship, but remember that passion is what makes your relationship unique. Are you looking for a business partner or a roommate? No. You're looking for the love of your life. It's your level of intimacy and bonding and continued attraction to each other that is the heat. I like to say it's the heat that melts the glue that keeps you together. It all plays into a baseline physical attraction like we talked about in the Black Hole of Mediocrity discussion. Someone can become more and more physically attractive as you get to know a beautiful personality. So find something you love to look at in that person. It can really get you through a tough day or an argument. You can be really mad, then look up and go, "Wow, I really do love that face." There's something really wonderful about that, and it's very powerful in maintaining your relationship. Of course it's tied into adoration and respect because what you really might be seeing is the sincerity or kindness in his eyes, and that's what makes you melt.

This also brings up the sometimes sensitive subject of our responsibility to take care of ourselves. I'm not talking about gaining a little weight or your body changing from having a baby or any of the normal things we go through as we get older. We have body changes, men can lose their hair, and even an accident can change how we look. This is not about having to be perfect or look 22 for the rest of your life. This is about taking care of yourself, from good hygiene to good cardiovascular health to maintaining your self-care, your self-respect and your self-esteem. Feeling sexy and attractive is a job for each of you. Because you are also *each bringing your own spark into the relationship*. (This is the subject of another entire book I'm writing on the subject of the Passion Triangle.) In short, he needs to take care of himself physically, mentally and emotionally the best he can and you do too. Yes, part of being in love is giving each other some room when life is hectic, but you don't want to enable each other to let things slide. The minute one of you starts to do something about it and feels healthier, more energetic and sexier, that person's going to suddenly become aware of how important that attraction thing is. If it's not there, it can chip away at your passion. So, too, can not bothering to look good for each other. It matters because it shows that you care about the fire being sparked and re-sparked. So let me be clear. You can have a need for him to let you know he finds you attractive and to share his response to your sexiness. That can be part of your love language and your dance. There's nothing wrong with that. But you can't rely on him to make you feel sexy. He is not the source of your sexiness, you are. And vice versa.

The fuel

This is essential for passion to last over time. You can have short-term passion with someone, but if you're not experiencing and developing a loving relationship, it's going to burn out. Remember RAW: respect, appreciation and warmth. Those are the things that make a man feel loved. You might have a different language for it, but those are the qualities of the kind of love I hope you also want to receive.

This part seems somewhat magical and part of the mystery of chemistry, but these are also feelings you can experience with many different people in your life. They might not combine with sexual attraction to make passion, but think about the people in your life you respect, appreciate and feel love for. Friendships and family relationships where you experience **authenticity** and **allegiance** are also the ones that feel most loving. Don't settle for anything less than that as a baseline for your chosen partner. Remember the Black Hole of Mediocrity: don't live there.

Building a nice stack of wood or "fuel" for the fire to continue burning requires an experience, over time, of authenticity and allegiance. Think about a casual, hook-up relationship: there is plenty of air, plenty of spark because it's novel, but the shared time together where you get to feel into being authentic with each other and having each other's back doesn't exist. So eventually it gets real old real fast. All the attraction in the world can't keep the fire burning. It's merely kindling.

The oxygen

This is actually the most important element of the fire to understand because it can be the most confusing. It's essential, however, in order to keep the passion burning. It's counterintuitive for many women to think that if a man loves you and wants you that he would be OK with being away from you. But, please hear me out on this. This is what makes you the object of his desire, not just for weeks, not for months, but for years and even decades. Think about a fire. You need heat to ignite it and fuel and oxygen to keep it burning. Easiest way to put out a candle? A snuffer. Take away the oxygen and you put out the fire.

Now think about fanning the flames and how that keeps a fire alive, feeding it oxygen and moving it towards more fuel. It's science.

It's natural law. You can't change it any more than you can change gravity. Any healthy male who tells you he doesn't want any space after the first month or so of constant togetherness is just being nice. Either that or he's afraid to tell you he wants it because he doesn't know how to express this without hurting your feelings. He could love being around you and may not even understand what it is that doesn't feel right. So many guys walk from relationships or label themselves afraid of commitment because commitment starts to be synonymous with smothering. And many are sad to have left a very loving woman because she was ultimately too loving.

Remember: men are visceral. They feel what they feel, and they don't try to convince themselves to feel any other way. So you might say, "Well how am I supposed to be authentic and give him space if that's just the way I am? I'm loving, I'm attentive, I'm affectionate. I want to be around him all the time. What if that's my truth? What's wrong with that?" Well, if you water a garden too much, you're going to kill it. And if you've gone from life without him to life with him, and now suddenly your life is all "him, him, him," let's be honest – you're forgetting some of your truth along the way. You have to be honest about how much of this is based in fear for you. Fear of him doing stuff without you, fear of him forgetting about you, fear of not being there for him, fear of somehow failing. It can also be fear of missing him because it simply doesn't feel good.

Let's go back to the dance and calibration. If you're playing the long game, you've got to do your life, not make it all about him and you have to create some breathing space in the relationship. Unlate so that you can relate. Get a hobby if you need to. See your friends. Go to the gym. You don't have to work out together. It's not your job to be available to him at a moment's notice. Let him have to figure out how he is going to get the pleasure of seeing you. That's half the fun for him.

For example, if you go out with your friends or you go away for the weekend and he says he misses you, that doesn't mean he's bummed and you should fix it. Don't fix him missing you, let him fix it. He needs to miss you. It's science. It's law. It's good for him. Err on the side of space, because, trust me, if there's something about your life and career that doesn't work for him because he truly doesn't see you enough, he will bring it up. He will start throwing out ideas to solve it. That's what they do. Just because he says, "I miss you," that does not translate to, "Never go away again." So don't change a thing. Just smile and say to yourself, "Good. You should miss me because I'm awesome," and then say to him, "I miss you too, handsome." Always encourage him to have fun. Don't insist that he miss you. Tell him to have fun with his friends. Tell him you're having a good time. There's nothing wrong with thinking, "Oh, I wish he could have tasted the eggs I had this morning." Share experiences, let him know you thought of him, but *nothing* that says, "I can't have a good time without you and you shouldn't have a good time without me." The reason you fell in love with each other is because you were both cool people, and cool people aren't half a person without their mate.

Two halves don't make a whole in this case. Two whole people make one awesome couple. A man who wants your whole identity to be in relation to him, who truly doesn't want any space, is an insecure man. You might think you want a guy who wants you around all the time until you realize that he's controlling and emotionally dangerous. At first, this can be mistaken for how much he must love you, but it's not based in love. It's based in fear. That's not the kind of guy you want to hang with.

Good men who love you still need air. They need room to breathe. They want the flame of passion to be fanned. You may or may not be in touch with your need for air too, but if you are, listen anyway. Sometimes, as women, when we need some space, we start thinking we're not in love. Like, "How can I not want to be around him?" But that doesn't necessarily mean anything of the sort. You might just be having an honest moment with yourself that says, "I need some space to think and breathe and miss this guy." That is totally healthy and probably tapping into your masculine energy a little bit, needing some linear focus. Or maybe you just miss your friends. It's all valid and healthy. Breathing room isn't just physical, it's mental too.

When I talk about mental breathing room, it really brings us all the way back around to authenticity. Being able to be yourself must include your passionate sexual self. Being able to be honest about your thoughts and desires around sex usually takes some time in a relationship, but that's going to go at its own pace. Embracing and sharing who we are sexually is a huge part of a whole other book, but what I will say about newly forming relationships, which is where we are focused in this book, is that I encourage you to create space for that kind of honesty by once again remembering it's one thing to have a problem or a boundary around someone's actions. It's another to shame them for their thoughts and desires. Stay curious. Stay interested. Remember your two new best friends: interest and curiosity. You and your partner are both expanding as people. Your relationship is expanding and your sex life needs to come along for the ride. Your sex life is the context. It's the forum of expression for your passion in your relationship, and it is a precious part of your relationship.

So keep it safe. Keep it loving. Keep it breathing. Keep the fire lit with the dance of attraction, loving acceptance and room to breathe both in your physical space and your psyche. When two whole people with room for expansion come together, that relationship becomes greater than the sum of its parts.

Recognizing aaah

Let's look at your PDF. Think back on your relationships that included some physical intimacy. I want you to reflect a little bit on the "aaah" part, the passion part. Did you feel all three elements (fuel, heat, air) of that passion and, if not, what was lacking? Was there anyone you felt a lot of love for, but maybe not heat? Were you lacking a spark? And was that right away or did that happen over time? Maybe all three elements were clicking, but the fire died out because someone smothered the air or because there wasn't quite enough attraction in the mix to keep it sparking. What would you do differently, if anything? Is there anyone in your life that had a degree of masculine energy that you really liked? It actually doesn't even have to be a lover. What did it feel like or what does it feel like to be around that person?

Does a man with a little more feminine energy soften you in a way that can be healthy for you? I know, because I have a lot of feminine energy, when I'm around secure, healthy, masculine energy, I feel grounded. I also feel like it's safe to express all my feminine energy no matter how chaotic it is – chaos isn't always a bad thing — because that person can handle it. So, for me, that's a very sexy feeling. If you've ever experienced that one way or the other, write down what that feels like for you.

Have you ever dealt with a long-distance relationship? Sometimes in a long-distance relationship you can experience heat and plenty of oxygen, but you start to realize there might not be enough love for fuel. Many people need actual presence and experience together to nurture that love part, so long-distance can be tricky that way. You have space and spark because you miss each other and you're attracted to each other, but it has trouble lasting over time because you're not feeding it with enough loving experience. Remember, love is not a feeling. Love is a verb. It's about being loving, with authenticity and allegiance. That's why a lot of long-distance relationships don't last in spite of the best intentions.

Aaah review

The three main elements of a real deal relationship that create stability, emotional safety and fertile ground for growth are authenticity, which is the ability to be yourself and let him be himself; allegiance, which is about being on the same team, being committed to each other's growth, and trusting each other's intent; and then there's "aaah," which is passion. And the law of passion follows the scientific law of the fire triangle, aka The Passion Triangle.™

To ignite a fire, you need heat, fuel and oxygen. Fuel and oxygen keep it burning and, frankly, create more heat which is the thing that starts that baby up over and over again. And that's how passion lasts for decades. But what's the most challenging element that keeps it burning over decades? Oxygen. Throughout much of this book, I've stressed the need to be loving, the importance of attraction and staying out of that Black Hole of Mediocrity. Here, however, we stress the importance of creating space, both mental and physical, because that is going to fan the flames of desire and passion.

Conclusion

● ● ● ● ● ●

Revisiting your vision statement

As your last bit of homework in this book, I invite you to pull out your list and vision statement or open that rough draft file. Remember, this is a living, breathing document like the constitution, something you can continually revisit. Add these three statements to the top of the list:

I attract someone I can be myself with.

I attract someone who has my back and cares about my growth and expansion.

I attract someone I have a ton of sexual chemistry with.

If you remind yourself of nothing more each and every day, it should be these three statements. I hope that you will read or record your vision statement and bask in the joy of your new story at least twice a week, but life happens and it's easy to forget. These three statements can be little Post-it notes on your mirror or a sign on your refrigerator, because you know the deeper meaning of them now and how these things look and feel in the context of your life and your specific desire for someone who compliments your life.

You don't have to settle for less than that because it's not too much to ask, especially when you're willing to give it in return. These are things that a real deal guy is totally capable of. They are out there and they want it too. Now that you know a little bit more about the man / woman dance, calibration and the need for oxygen, you can have a good man who's not only in love with you, but passionate about you. If you get intentional about having these three things, authenticity, allegiance and aaah, a lot of that other stuff on your list becomes fluid and flexible. To be your whole self with someone who adores you, has your back and rocks your world with proper amounts of lust and respect – *that* is the real deal.

Resources and Recommended Reading

• • • • • •

Breaking the Habit of Being Yourself by Dr. Joe Dispenza

You Can Heal Your Life by Louise L. Hay

The Power of Now by Eckhart Tolle

The Law of Attraction by Esther and Jerry Hicks

The Road Less Traveled by M. Scott Peck

I Hope I Screw This Up by Kyle Cease

Anatomy of the Spirit by Caroline Myss, PhD

The Four Agreements by Don Miguel Ruiz

The Seven Spiritual Laws of Success by Deepak Chopra

40 Day Mind Fast Soul Feast by Michael Beckwith

Nonviolent Communication by Marshall B. Rosenberg, PhD

The Power of Intention by Wayne Dyer

Coaching and support information available at sophievenable.com.

Intentional Dating PDFs available in my free resource library. Use email opt-in at sophievenable.com

In Gratitude

● ● ● ● ● ●

This book would not exist without my clients. Your courage and commitment to the process of opening up to a healthy version of love is what has inspired me to share this information. Your joy is my joy and I am honored to have been a part of your journey.

Writing the original curriculum 4 years ago began with Katarina Rocha. Thank you for letting me "teach" to you and untangle all those darn learning objectives. Your patience and encouragement truly helped me get it done.

Sheena DuPonte for your coaching, encouragement, friendship and love. Seriously.

Brad Holliday, thank you for going over all of the material from your wise and loving male perspective and for always believing in me.

Marina Braff, my ultimate friend and colleague, living and testing and living and proving and living some more! Thank you for wearing all of the hats you have worn in my life.

Jodi Schecter, your support and encouragement has been invaluable, my friend.

Natalie Susi, first and foremost, I am grateful for your friendship. But I would feel a lost without your read-throughs and generous time spent on this and other works. The Universe hooked us up and I feel lucky!

Kirstyn Smith, thank you for your editing expertise as well as your encouraging, kind words. You were a delight to work with.

Florence Cao, for your cover and interior design... and patience! So happy to have found you.

Mark, for inspiring all of this. The way you believe in me is humbling. I love you.

My girls, Julia and Natalie, for inspiring and challenging me. You are both so wise and beautiful. If I have only ever helped you to choose big love, then my time here is well spent.

Made in USA - North Chelmsford, MA
1062455_9781692617431
03.25.2020 1107